You Don't Have to Wear a Denim Jumper to Homeschool

*A Practical Guide for
Real Families Who Just Want to
Teach Their Kids at Home*

By **LAUREN YOUNG**

For God,
because none of this happens without Him.

For my husband, who loves me even when
I drag him into my latest crazy idea.

For my kids, who remind me daily
that homeschooling is both a blessing
and an adventure.

And for the parents reading this who wonder
if you're "qualified." You are.

Dear Reader

If you're holding this book, chances are you're thinking about homeschooling — or maybe you're already in it, wondering if anyone else feels this crazy. (Good news: You're not alone.)

Maybe you grew up thinking homeschoolers all wore denim jumpers and made their own soap.
Maybe you're worried you're not organized enough, patient enough, or "good enough."
Maybe you're trying to figure out if you can actually do this without losing your mind — or your sense of humor.

Wherever you are in the journey, I want you to hear this loud and clear:
You can do this — exactly as you are.

You don't need to change who you are.
You don't need to fit a stereotype.
You don't need a perfect plan.

What you do need is a little courage, a little flexibility, and a whole lot of grace (for yourself and your kids).

This isn't a rulebook. It's not a manual.
It's a conversation.
A pep talk.
A real-life guide from someone who's been there —
and who still sometimes teaches in pajamas.

I'm here to walk with you, laugh with you, and remind you that homeschooling isn't about being perfect — it's about being present.

And just in case you were still wondering —
No, you don't have to wear a denim jumper to homeschool.
(But if you want to, no judgment. Extra pockets are always a win.)

Let's get started.
– Lauren

Table of Contents

Part 1: So You're Thinking About Homeschooling... 10

CHAPTER 1: Congratulations (or Condolences?)
Deciding to Homeschool Without Losing Your Mind.....11

CHAPTER 2: Myths That Need to Die
*You don't need a farm, 15 kids, or a degree
in everything... 19*

CHAPTER 3: Start Where You Are
Why You're Already Qualified (Yes, Even You)...........33

Part 2: Building Your Homeschool Life........................ 42

CHAPTER 4: What School Really Looks Like
at Home *Spoiler:
It Doesn't Take 7 Hours a Day....................................... 43*

CHAPTER 5: Curriculum Panic:
Choosing Without Crying
How to Pick What Works (and Ditch What Doesn't).....49

CHAPTER 6: Schedules, Rhythms,
and Other Mythical Creatures
Finding a Flow that Fits Your Family............................ 59

CHAPTER 7: Groups, Co-Ops, and Socialization
AKA, "Will My Kid Have Friends?"..................................... 73

CHAPTER 8: The Beauty of Pajama Days
Learning Doesn't Always Look Like Pen and Paper..... 83

Part 3: Handling the Hard Stuff...92

CHAPTER 9: When It's Hard (Because It Will Be)
Slowing Down, Speeding Up, and Staying Sane........ 93

CHAPTER 10: Testing, Grading, and Other
Things You Don't Have to Fear
Keeping Track Without Losing Sight......................... 103

CHAPTER 11: Transcripts, High School Credits,
and Graduation
You're Not Too Late to Do This..................................... 111

CHAPTER 12: When the Journey Looks Different
*Special Needs, Learning Differences,
and Homeschooling with Heart*................................. 125

CHAPTER 13: Faith in the Middle
*Why the Messy Middle Matters
More Than You Think*.. 135

Part 4: Bonus Life Lessons They Don't Tell You............ 144

CHAPTER 14: Instagram Lies and Real-Life Wins
Comparison is the Thief of Joy (and Sanity)............ 145

CHAPTER 15: Permission Slips You Didn't Know You Needed
Yes, You Can Take a Day Off. Yes, You Can Change Plans.................................155

CHAPTER 16: The Real Goal of All of This
Raising Thinkers, Dreamers, Doers, and Disciples......161

Extras: 168

A Letter to the Homeschool Mom Who's Still Not Sure
(Because You Might Need to Hear It Twice).....................169

Rapid-Fire FAQ
(Because You Might Still Wonder...) 173

Acknowledgments 179

Part I:

So You're Thinking About Homeschooling...

CHAPTER 1:

Congratulations (or Condolences?)

Deciding to Homeschool Without Losing Your Mind

Well, here you are.

You're either seriously thinking about homeschooling, have already signed yourself up for it, or have accidentally ended up Googling "how to homeschool without losing your mind." (Welcome. You're among friends.)

First of all — congratulations.
Or maybe…condolences.
Honestly, it depends on the day.

Because homeschooling?

> It's one of the most beautiful, life-changing, occasionally hair-pulling journeys you'll ever take.

It will stretch you, humble you, delight you, and yes — on certain afternoons — it might just send you to the pantry clutching a half-eaten brownie, a thousand-yard stare, and a mental draft of your resignation letter.

And that's normal.

Here's the deal:
You don't have to be a superhero to homeschool your kids.
You don't have to have a fully organized color-coded binder system, a degree in education, a classical music playlist queued up, or — let's all say it together — a denim jumper.

You just need to show up.
You need to care enough to try —
even on the messy days.
And maybe have a sense of humor about the whole thing, because trust me, you're going to need it.

This isn't about creating the "perfect" homeschool. It's about creating a life where your kids can learn, grow, question, explore, mess up, try again, and (eventually) fly.

It's about real education for real people.

In this book, we're going to talk about all the things I wish someone had told me when I started out — the myths I believed, the mistakes I made, and the massive amount of grace I had to learn to give myself (and my kids).

We'll cover everything from what a normal homeschool day looks like (spoiler: it's not 7 hours of worksheets) to how to pick a curriculum without crying into your Dr. Pepper at midnight after doom-scrolling 4,385,305,584 curriculum options.

Or worse — accidentally wandering into a massive homeschool convention where everyone else seemed to know what they were doing while you were just trying to figure out if "unit study" was a brand or a religion.

We'll talk about groups, co-ops, transcripts, graduation, doubts, burnouts, pajama days, and everything in between.

Bottom line?
You can do this.
You don't have to be perfect — you just have to be present.
And if you happen to be present in yoga pants and yesterday's mascara — or, let's be honest, full-on pajamas — well…welcome to the club.

Let's dive in.

But before we dive in, let me tell you a little bit about how I got here.

I wasn't someone who always dreamed of homeschooling.
In fact, I have a teaching degree.
I used it for exactly one year — teaching middle schoolers — before I had my first child and decided to stay home.

At some point, I did think about homeschooling…but I quickly realized it wasn't for me.
I loved teaching, sure — but I liked teaching other people's kids.
And older ones.
Not my own toddlers, who thought crayons were a food group.
Not my own kindergartener, who needed three costume changes before math.

Homeschooling felt like a nice idea for other people — people who were more patient, more organized, or maybe just more brave.
Not me.

We had it made.
My kids were in an amazing school — K4 through 12th grade, classically based (just what we wanted), filled with incredible people, and a place where they were thriving, learning, and loving every minute of it.
I loved it too. I loved dropping them off, loved my "me time," loved seeing them grow and succeed.

Everything was…perfect.

Until it wasn't.

I started to feel it creeping in — the sadness when I dropped them off.
The way the house felt too quiet.
The feeling that I was missing something I wasn't supposed to miss.

At first, I ignored it.
When my wonderful friend Meagan kept saying maybe I should homeschool, I laughed in her face. (Like, real, borderline rude laughing.)
This wasn't for me. No way. No how.

But somewhere along the way, the laughter turned into late-night phone calls — the ugly cry kind — where I whispered, "Am I crazy? Could I actually do this?"

It made no sense.
I couldn't recreate what their school was doing.
I couldn't teach them everything they were learning.
I couldn't possibly give them the same experiences.
Was I going to ruin everything they had worked so hard for?
Was I going to hold them back?
NO THANK YOU.

I told myself it wasn't for me.
I told myself I was confused.
I told myself God wasn't calling me to this.

And yet...I couldn't shake it.

Then came Christmas break.
It was the best Christmas we'd ever had.
Slow mornings. Long talks. Belly laughs. Real connection.

And for the first time, I realized:
I didn't want to send them back.

I went to youth group (I was a leader at the time) and, true to form, unloaded all my tears, doubts, and drama on Meagan — my unofficial homeschool counselor, sounding board, and personal saint — who by this point deserved to be sainted, knighted, given her own national holiday, and probably skip the line at the pearly gates just for putting up with me.
Once more, I walked away saying, "Nope. Not for me."

I left church that night, got halfway home — and had to pull over.
I was physically sick from the turmoil inside me.

That's when my husband said something that changed everything:

"I'm here for whatever you decide…but you have to decide. The stress of sitting in the middle is killing you."

So, halfway scared to death, I halfway decided to homeschool.
We told the school we more than likely wouldn't be returning the next year.

And then…

COVID hit.

Homeschooling wasn't just a choice anymore — it was in my lap.
Ready or not, I was doing it.

And you know what?
We never looked back.

CHAPTER 2:

Myths That Need to Die

*You don't need a farm, 15 kids,
or a degree in everything.*

Before we get any further, we need to deal with something:
The Myths.

The second you tell someone you're thinking about homeschooling — or the second you dare to even think about it yourself — you're going to run straight into a wall of bad assumptions, well-meaning advice, and horror stories someone's aunt's neighbor's cousin told them once.

And if you're anything like me, you might have a few myths rattling around in your own head, too.

Let's bust them now, before they have a chance to stick.

Myth #1: You Have to Be a Certified Teacher to Homeschool

Bless it.
If I had a dollar for every time someone said, "But... you're not a teacher!"
Guess what? You are now.

Now — full disclosure — I do have a teaching degree. I taught middle school for a year before deciding to stay home with my babies.

But let me tell you a little secret:
When it comes to homeschooling, my degree has been way less helpful than the wisdom of the dozens of mamas I homeschool alongside — most of whom don't have degrees.

You've been teaching your kids since the day they were born.
If you survived potty training, you can survive long division.

> Real-life, real-world experience, heart, and a willingness to learn right alongside your kids will take you farther than any certification ever could.

Myth #2: You Have to Recreate Public School at Home

NOPE.

Homeschooling doesn't mean setting up little desks in rows, teaching math at 9:00 sharp, and switching subjects every 45 minutes while blowing a whistle. (Unless you want to. No judgment. Whistles can be fun.)

A real homeschool day might look like math at the kitchen table, science experiments on the porch, reading snuggled on the couch, and a history discussion while someone's still in pajamas.

And here's something else no one tells you:
You don't have to do every subject every single day.
History? Science? Social studies?
Those can easily be done one or two days a week — and your kids will still learn plenty.
You don't have to cram every topic into every day.

Homeschooling is a marathon, not a sprint — and it's a lot more flexible than you think.

The beauty of homeschooling is that you aren't tied to a clock — or a bell — or a checklist.
You get to build something better: a life where learning fits into living.

And let's be honest — most of us didn't choose this because we wanted our house to look like a school.

We chose it because something *wasn't working*.
So why would we try to recreate the very thing we walked away from?

Trying to homeschool like a traditional classroom is like putting a sparkly saddle on a cow and entering it in the Kentucky Derby.
It's not going to run faster.
It's going to get frustrated, refuse to move, and probably poop on your boots.

> You weren't called to copy. You were called to create.

So ditch the guilt, burn the fake schedule, and let go of the idea that your homeschool has to look like anyone else's — including a school's.
You've got freedom here.
Use it well.

Myth #3: Your Kids Will Turn Out Weird

First of all — define "weird."
Because honestly, if not being obsessed with TikTok dances and cafeteria drama is weird...I'm fine with it.

Homeschooled kids aren't doomed to be socially awkward hermits who knit their own underwear by age 12. Although, if they did, you'd have some seriously useful Christmas gifts.

Here's the thing — this whole idea that homeschooling automatically ruins your child's social skills?
It's based on the assumption that being surrounded by a bunch of kids the *exact same age* in a peer-driven environment is what creates social maturity.
Spoiler: It doesn't.

If anything, it teaches kids how to survive in a bubble of same-age pressure — where "fitting in" matters more than forming real, lasting character.

Who teaches kids how to *actually* navigate social situations with grace, confidence, and maturity if they're not regularly around people older and wiser than them?
The answer?
No one.
There's a reason *peer pressure* is a term we all know. It's what happens when immature people are left to teach each other how to be... less immature. And it rarely ends in wisdom.

Socialization in homeschooling just looks different.
It's conversations with real people of all ages — not just kids born the same year.
It's helping an elderly neighbor rake leaves.
It's reading aloud to toddlers at church.

It's co-op classes, sports teams, science fairs, youth groups, family trips, dinner table debates, and learning how to carry on a conversation that doesn't start with "what grade are you in?"

In short?
It's **real life**.

And real life is a much better training ground for adulthood than memorizing where to sit at the cool table.

Myth #4: Crisis Schooling Was the Same as Homeschooling

Let's set the record straight right now:
COVID crisis schooling was NOT homeschooling.

When schools shut down during COVID, families were thrown into a whirlwind.
There was chaos. Confusion.
Packets being emailed at midnight. Zoom calls freezing while your toddler drew on the walls.

That was not homeschooling.
That was emergency survival schooling — trying to replicate a broken system during a global crisis with zero warning or support.

Homeschooling, on the other hand, is intentional.
It's crafted around your family's rhythms, needs, values, and goals.

It's not just "public school at home" — it's a completely different mindset and lifestyle.

So if you had a bad taste in your mouth after COVID schooling, please know:

> You weren't made to copy the system. You were made to do something better.

That wasn't homeschooling.

Not even close.

And remember *Myth #2* — trying to recreate the traditional school model at home is the fastest way to burn out.

Myth #5: Homeschoolers Fall Behind Academically

Let's be real.
Some homeschoolers are behind in math.
Some public schoolers are behind in math.
Some private schoolers are behind in math.
Some adults are behind in math.
(Hi. It's me. I am some adults.)

I am horrible at math.
Big shoutout to Nicole, the Math Lady for being the real MVP. (Can I get an amen?)

Seriously, there are amazing resources out there — and you do not have to be a walking calculator to homeschool successfully.

Here's what matters:

- Is your child learning?
- Is your child growing?
- Is your child being challenged and supported in ways that actually fit who they are — not just where someone thinks they should be by age 8.5?

Homeschooling allows you to tailor education to real learning, not just checking boxes. Sometimes that means racing ahead. Sometimes that means slowing way down and getting it solid.

> Falling "behind" is a moving target depending on who's holding the measuring stick.

And both are wins.

Myth #6: I Have to Know Everything Before I Start

Spoiler:
You won't.
Ever.

And that's the beauty of it.

Homeschooling isn't about standing at a whiteboard like you're the all-knowing keeper of facts.
(Do we even need whiteboards? We don't even have desks most of the time.)

It's about learning with your kids.

Honestly?
I learn new things all the time alongside mine.
My husband even jokes that homeschooling the kids has been the best thing that ever happened to me!
And honestly...he's not wrong.

Trivia nights at restaurants have gotten a lot more fun. And I'm finally converting some fractions in the kitchen without asking Siri, Alexa, or whatever AI assistant is closest to my phone. (Progress, people. Progress.)

The truth is, homeschooling isn't about having all the answers.
It's about modeling curiosity, perseverance, and humility.

If you can say,
"*I don't know — but let's find out together,*"
you're already homeschooling exactly right.

Also, shoutout to Google, library cards, YouTube, Nicole the Math Lady, and every bookstore bargain bin. Help is literally everywhere.

Myth #7: You Can't Work and Homeschool

Listen, working and homeschooling isn't easy — but it's absolutely possible.
Thousands of families do it every single day, in every kind of setup you can imagine.

- Some work part-time.
- Some work from home.
- Some split the teaching load with a spouse or a grandparent.
- Some build flexible schedules that fit around early mornings, evenings, or weekends.
- Some lean into independent learning as kids get older.

Me?
I work.
I co-own a homeschool group with a friend (shoutout to Apex!), and I have side hustles that let me work from home or arrange my schedule around our life.

It doesn't mean I have endless free time.
It means our homeschool days — and honestly, our homeschool weeks — almost never look the same.

Sometimes we're schooling in the morning, sometimes in the afternoon.
Sometimes we cram a full week into four days.
Sometimes life demands we take a detour, and we adjust.

But hey — what a life skill my kids are learning: how to go with the flow.
(Also known as "how to survive adulthood without losing your mind.")

And it's not just me working either.
Our kids work too!

They're only 12 and 13, but they show cows — a commitment that takes a ton of hard work, traveling, care, and discipline.
Homeschooling gives them the freedom to pursue passions and responsibilities at the same time.

So, yes — you can homeschool and work.
Your kids can homeschool and work too.
Real life. Real skills. Real preparation for the future.

Is it hard sometimes? Yep.
Does it take creativity, flexibility, and a sense of humor? Absolutely.

But if you feel called to homeschool and still need (or want) to work, don't count yourself out.

I know what you're thinking:
"Wait a second. The tagline said you don't have to have a farm, 15 kids, or a degree...but you have a farm and a degree."

Okay, fair.
But let's be clear:
The farm came after the homeschooling.

And it's not like we're running some giant ranch out here — we have a few show cows, a handful of chickens, and one duck who is absolutely convinced she's a chicken.

> There's not just one right way to homeschool. There's the right way for your family.

We just roll with it. She fits right in.

And as for the 15 kids part?
Nope.
We had two — and said, "That'll do."

Bottom line?
You absolutely do not have to live in the middle of nowhere, have a teaching license hanging on your wall, or run a petting zoo to homeschool successfully.

You just have to love your kids, be willing to learn, and trust that God equips those He calls.

And if you're here, reading this?
You're already on your way.

CHAPTER 3:

Start Where You Are

Why You're Already Qualified (Yes, Even You)

If you're waiting for the perfect time to start homeschooling...
You're going to be waiting a long time.

There's never a perfect time.
There's never a perfect curriculum, a perfect house, a perfect plan, or a perfect season.

There's just you, your kids, and today.
And that's more than enough.

You don't need a Pinterest-worthy homeschool room.
Our homeschool space is wherever we find a clean table — or a cleared-off corner of the couch.

You don't need a color-coded daily schedule with fifteen different fonts.
We use a glorified checklist...when we remember.

You don't need a four-year master plan, a whiteboard wall, or a fancy monogrammed bookbag complete with color-coded binders and built-in snack compartments.
(Okay...maybe the monogrammed bookbag. This Southern girl will slap a monogram on anything that holds still long enough.)

You also don't need a laminator, a binding machine, or one of those giant paper cutters that looks like it could take out a small village.
Although, if you happen to have one...respect.

Here's what you do need:

- A willing heart.
- A little courage.
- A Bible in your hand.
- Your "Why"
- And the humility to learn as you go.

That's it.

Start where you are.
Right now.

With the house you have, the books you can borrow, the Bible you can open, the schedule that mostly works, the kids in front of you, and the faith that God equips those He calls.

What's Your Why?

You need to know **why** you're homeschooling.

Not just "I want more time with my kids" or "Public school wasn't a good fit" — though those are valid.
But deep down, soul-level *why*.
The kind you can cling to when everything feels like it's falling apart.

Ask yourself:
• What do I want my kids to remember about this season?
• What do I hope they become because of this experience?
• What matters most to our family?

Write it down.
Tuck it in your planner.
Stick it to your fridge.
Put it wherever you'll see it when the tears hit, the doubt creeps in, or the math book flies across the room.

Because your *why* won't change every time the day gets hard.

But it *will* help you remember why you're still showing up.

But What If I'm Totally Unprepared?

Spoiler:
We all are.

Everyone feels unprepared when they start.
And honestly, we all still feel unprepared sometimes... even years in.

You're stepping into a new adventure — of course, you don't have it all figured out yet.
But here's the thing:
You don't have to.

You learn by doing.
You figure it out while you're doing it.
You adjust and shift and tweak and laugh and sometimes cry — and then you get up and do it again.
And slowly, you find your rhythm.

The good news?

> God's not looking for perfect homeschool parents. He's looking for willing ones.

It's Okay to Start Small

You don't have to launch into homeschooling with all twelve subjects and a full marching band. (Actually...please don't.)

Start with a few basics:

- Bible.
- Reading.
- Writing.
- Math.

Time together.
Conversations that matter.
Books that spark questions.
Walks around the neighborhood that turn into science lessons.
Laughing when the experiment explodes.
Pausing when the tears come.
Picking back up when you're ready.

Start with a Story
If you're looking for something easy *and* impactful, start here: **read aloud.**

That's it. A library trip. A book off the shelf. A quick Amazon order.
No laminator required.

Reading aloud — even just a few minutes a day — can be one of the simplest ways to connect, calm the chaos, and open the door to big conversations. And when you choose books *above* your child's reading level? You stretch their minds, grow their vocabulary, and spark the kind of deep learning that lasts.

"Frequent family reading has been linked to higher academic achievement, stronger emotional regulation, and increased empathy — even into adolescence."
(*Source: American Academy of Pediatrics & various longitudinal studies*)

Reading aloud doesn't just build better readers — it builds better *humans*.
And it keeps hearts close, long after they're reading on their own.

Small starts grow into big things

When COVID hit, I was scrambling to come up with anything to keep us going.

We had pulled our kids from school after that "a couple weeks' break" turned into "we have no idea when we're going back."
We already knew we were going to homeschool the following year, so we figured — why not just go ahead and finish this one out on time?

One day, desperate for something educational that didn't involve another worksheet, I printed a bingo-style scavenger hunt list of things to find outside. We loaded up in the side-by-side, spent the afternoon bouncing around the property checking off the list... and then came back inside and googled most of what we found — because honestly, I had no clue how to explain half of it.

And guess what?
It was enough.

Confession Time:
My Type A (and Type D?) Start

Now, you should know something about me:
I can be extremely Type A.
And sometimes...Type D? It's way past B, whatever it is.
Thanks, ADHD.

So naturally, when I decided to homeschool, I thought I needed it all.

Off we went to IKEA, ready to completely transform the bonus room over our garage into the ultimate classroom.

We bought desks.
Chairs.
Painted wooden letters with the kids' names perfectly hung above each desk — color-coordinated, of course,

to their matching work folders.
I even had a teacher desk — fully stocked with every tool, supply, and organizational system I could dream of (and would certainly never need).

And the schedule?
Oh, I had a schedule.
Every single day was planned down to the minute — from 9:00 a.m. to 2:30 p.m. sharp.

See?
This is where that teaching degree can actually hurt you.
I was still stuck in the mindset of what "real school" was supposed to look like.

We had the setup.
We had the structure.
We had all the "right" things.

And off we went...

Guess what?

We hated it.

(There's a lot more to the story of how we eventually started loving homeschooling — and we'll get there. But just know: stuff, schedules, and perfect setups don't automatically make learning beautiful.)

Real Talk: What Starting Looked Like for Us

When we actually found our footing, it didn't look like a Pinterest classroom.
It looked like a dining room table that doubled as a science lab, a spelling station, a lunch counter, and sometimes a jungle gym.

We didn't have a perfect curriculum lineup.
We had a handful of books, a lot of Amazon deliveries (because the library was closed tighter than Fort Knox in early 2020), and even more trial and error.

Some days felt amazing.
Some days felt like a disaster.

But every day — every single day — we were building something.

Brick by brick.
Memory by memory.
Conversation by conversation.

And I wouldn't trade it for anything.

Part II:

Building Your Homeschool Life

CHAPTER 4:

What School Really Looks Like at Home

Spoiler: It Doesn't Take 7 Hours a Day

Spoiler alert:
Homeschooling isn't public school at home.
It's a whole different world — and yes, the snacks are better and the dress code is optional.

Forget the picture in your head of rows of desks, worksheets flying, a recess whistle blowing at exactly 10:15, and a PE teacher yelling at your kids to run laps in the backyard.

It's math at the kitchen table while someone eats their third breakfast.
It's reading on the couch while the dog

> Real homeschool life?
> It looks a lot more like real life.

climbs over everybody.

It's science experiments in the backyard because you're not about to clean baking soda off your ceiling again.

It's history discussions in the car on the way to show cows.

It's spelling practice while you're making dinner, because why not multitask?

It's Bible time on the porch swing.

It's messy, flexible, hilarious, sometimes frustrating... and absolutely beautiful.

You Don't Have to "Do School" All Day

One of the biggest shocks when you start homeschooling?

It doesn't take 7 hours a day.

(And if it does, you're doing it wrong — or you're trying to teach and survive a toddler at the same time, in which case you deserve a trophy and a nap.)

Homeschooling is focused learning, not "fill all the hours" learning.

When you're not wrangling 25 kids into bathroom lines, handing out worksheets, and taking attendance, you get a lot more done... a lot faster.

Here's a little reality check:

- → Most elementary kids can finish their core work in 2-3 hours.
- → Middle schoolers might need 3-4 hours.
- → High schoolers around 4-5 hours, depending on their workload and independence.

That's it.
Seriously.

The rest of the day?
It's free for field trips, hobbies, sports, reading, art, working cows, baking cookies, stacking rocks, getting muddy, helping neighbors, chasing chickens, or just being a kid.

No Two Days Look the Same (And That's Okay)

Here's another secret:
You won't have a perfect "Monday through Friday" schedule.

Some days will go exactly like you planned.
Some days will derail by 9:17 a.m., and you'll wonder if you should just start over tomorrow.

Both days are part of homeschooling.
Both days are wins.

Some weeks, we school hard Monday through Thursday and leave Friday for adventures.

Some weeks, we flex around travel for livestock shows, field trips, dentist appointments, and random Tuesday mornings when nobody can brain. Some weeks, we cram a whole science unit into one giant Saturday experiment day.

(Some weeks, we do none of those things and survive on prayer, sarcasm, and a suspicious amount of drive-thru runs.)

That's life.
And honestly?
It's great preparation for adulthood — learning to manage real schedules, real interruptions, and real flexibility.

Real Learning Happens Everywhere

Real learning doesn't just happen at a desk.
It happens everywhere.

> The beauty of homeschooling is that the whole world becomes your classroom.

The kitchen teaches math.
(And yes — thanks to homeschooling, my kitchen math has actually improved. You're welcome, fraction conversions.)

The yard teaches agriculture.
(Show cows don't feed themselves, and neither do those stubborn chickens.)

The car rides teach history — or sometimes literature, thanks to audiobooks (and the fact that I start tossing out discussion questions while they're trapped and can't escape).

The grocery store teaches economics.
(And possibly emotional budgeting strategies when bacon costs $11.99.)

The laundry, the dishes, the chores?
That's home economics, baby.

And the Bible?
It teaches everything that actually matters.

Real homeschooling isn't about fitting life around school.

It's about letting *life* be the school.

And honestly?
That's the good stuff.

It's not about doing *everything*.
It's about doing the *right* things — on purpose.
It's about being intentional.
That's where the real learning lives.

CHAPTER 5:
Curriculum Panic: Choosing Without Crying

*How to Pick What Works
(and Ditch What Doesn't)*

Let's be real:
If there's anything that can send a brand-new homeschooler into a full-blown spiral, it's choosing curriculum.

The endless options.
The conflicting reviews.
The glossy catalogs (sooo pretty, sooo dangerous).
The terrifying price tags.
The feeling that if you choose wrong, your child will end up living in your basement forever, unable to calculate a tip or spell "Wednesday."

(And yes, for the record, I still have to say "Wed-nes-day" in my head every single time I spell it.)

Take a breath.
Choosing curriculum is important, yes — but it's not a forever decision, and it's not a you-must-get-this-right-on-the-first-try-or-else-you-are-doomed situation.

It's Like Grocery Shopping When You're Hungry

Picking a curriculum is like grocery shopping when you're hungry:
You think you're making great choices.
You feel responsible. Inspired. Prepared.

And then you unpack the bags and realize you bought a cart full of charcuterie and artisan jams... and forgot bread, milk, and anything remotely resembling a meal. (But hey, GIRL DINNER.)

That's curriculum shopping.
Everything looks necessary until you realize you bought an entire unit on medieval sword fighting... but forgot to teach grammar.

If what you picked doesn't end up fitting?
You adjust.
You swap it out.
You move on.

It's not failure — it's normal.

You're Not Marrying It

Repeat after me:
Curriculum is not your spouse.

You are not stuck with it forever.
You are allowed to switch if it isn't working.

You are allowed to tweak it, dump it, sell it, shelve it, loan it, burn it (kidding... mostly), or use it creatively to fit your family.

> Some of our best homeschooling years have been built on the bones of curriculums we abandoned halfway through. Been there.

Been there. Bought the t-shirt. Burned the math book.

Case in Point

We once used a math curriculum that was amazing — for a while.
It had great video lessons: short, clear, easy to follow... until it wasn't.

The videos taught the concept — but that was it.
No extra practice videos.
No quick tips.
No help when things went sideways.

So my kids would finish the video, look at me for help...
and I would be staring right back at them like,
"Y'all better phone a friend, because I am not the one!"

As I've already mentioned, math is not my strong suit.
It's getting better thanks to learning alongside my kids
— but trust me, it's been a journey.

We started drowning.
The kids were frustrated and stuck.
The lessons started dragging on forever.

Then came the grading — and trying to figure out
where they went wrong — while I sat there feeling
overstimulated, overwhelmed, and like a total failure.

And then one day, I remembered:
We don't have to keep doing this.

We closed the books and never opened them again.

A lot of our friends were using Nicole the Math Lady,
so we hopped over there — and it has been AMAZING.

She teaches concepts clearly.
She has tips and tricks, one-minute tutorials, funny
moments that keep the kids engaged, and — best part
— it grades everything for me.

(Insert angel choir sounds here.)

No, I'm not getting paid, getting kickbacks, or getting free subscriptions. She doesn't even know who this Southern mama is. We just love it that much.

And guess what?
My kids are learning.

I'm breathing.
Math isn't ruining our day anymore.

> Curriculum is a tool, not a chain.

Use what helps.
Toss what doesn't.

You're building an education, not auditioning for Curriculum Loyalty of the Year.

Shiny Catalog Syndrome (Ask Me How I Know)

When I first started, I ordered all the shiny catalogs. (Like, all of them.)

I sat there, highlighter in hand, dog-earing every page like I was studying for the Bar Exam.

I highlighted entire sections.
I made dream lists.
I mapped out imaginary school days where we would fit in phonics, Latin, Greek, Shakespeare, home economics, woodworking, fencing, underwater basket weaving, and maybe a little algebra just for fun.

And in my head?
It was all going to fit into a neat, beautiful day from 9:00 a.m. to 2:30 p.m., with happy, smiling, well-rounded children who never once argued over who got the last marker.

Reality check:
It would have taken approximately 30,384.5 hours a day to teach all the things I highlighted.

Eventually, I scaled it way back.
I ordered WAY less.

And even then?
I still have unopened workbooks buried in a closet.
I still find shiny curriculum I tried once and then listed for resale at 20% of what I paid for it.

And even then, people would lowball me like, "Will you take $5 and a Starbucks gift card?" 😒

Honestly? Keep your $5. Hand over the coffee.

I also realized that half the "extras" I was so worried about missing came naturally in everyday life — without needing a $1500 deluxe cross-curricular unit study on the life cycle of a frog.

What You Actually Need (At the Beginning)

Especially if you're just starting out, here's what you actually need:

- → Math
- → Language Arts (Reading, Writing, Spelling)
- → A few good books for history and science (and your library card... or, let's be real, your Amazon Prime account)
- → The Bible

That's it.
Truly.

Not ten electives.
Not three foreign languages.
Not a timeline project that takes over your living room wall with color-coded sticky notes.

The Basics Are Enough

I realized pretty quickly that all the extras I thought would be fun were just overwhelming all of us.

The kids had too much to do.
We could never truly enjoy anything because we were rushing to the next subject, the next project, the next box to check.

They were exhausted.
I was flustered and frustrated because no matter how much we did, I felt like I wasn't giving them enough.

It wasn't joyful.
It wasn't peaceful.
And it definitely wasn't the life we had wanted when we chose to homeschool.

When You Focus on Building Strong Readers, Writers, and Thinkers...

Everything else starts to fall into place naturally.

The extras grow out of curiosity and everyday life — not panic and pressure.

Start simple.
Stay sane.
Add sparkle later.

Quick Note Before We Move On

If you're homeschooling older kids, you might have certain subjects they have to take to meet graduation requirements where you live.
(Think algebra, biology, government, foreign language — the fun stuff.)

And yes, those things matter.
We want our kids to have every door open to them.

But even when you're navigating credits and requirements, the heart of it stays the same:

→ Stick to what's needed.
→ Focus on the basics.
→ Don't drown yourself (or your teenager) trying to cram in seventeen extra electives just because you saw a shiny ad or panicked at 2 a.m.

Cover what's required.
Cover what's foundational.

Then breathe.

You're still allowed to keep it simple, even in high school.

However — you're also allowed to add on and fluff up your day when you're ready and feel more comfortable.
We'll stick to the basics for now — and later, when the time is right, we'll talk about how to sprinkle in more.

Baby steps, not burnout.

CHAPTER 6:

Schedules, Rhythms, and Other Mythical Creatures

Finding a Flow that Fits Your Family

Take a deep breath.
If you came here looking for a color-coded schedule that runs like a Swiss watch for 180 days straight, you're about to be very disappointed.

(Spoiler: That's a mythical creature. Like unicorns. And kids who never lose pencils.)

Finding a homeschool flow isn't about building a rigid schedule that cracks under the first sick day, field trip, or toddler tantrum.
It's about building a rhythm — something flexible, sustainable, and life-giving.

It's about crafting a daily and weekly life that fits your family... not cramming your family into a mold you saw online.

Goodbye, guilt.
Hello, freedom.

No Chasing the Clock

> One of the most beautiful gifts of homeschooling is that you're not ruled by a clock.

You're not racing bells.
You're not panicking because it's 8:02 and someone forgot their shoes.

You can slow down if the day is hard.
You can push things off to tomorrow if you need more time.
You can skip ahead when a concept clicks easily.
You can even go out on a random school night — and nobody's handing you a tardy slip the next morning.

I'll never forget the night it really clicked for us.
Back when my daughter was younger, she was deep into competitive cheer — before she fell in love with cows.

One night after cheer practice, we met up with some friends to hang out and enjoy some local food trucks.

We sat outside, eating ice cream, laughing with friends, and watching our kids run wild with other homeschool families under the lights.

It was one of those simple, perfect nights.

A couple of strangers walked by, smiled,
and casually joked,
"Good luck getting all those kids up for school tomorrow morning after a late night and ice cream!"

I smiled and said,
"Oh, they can sleep in. We'll start a little later — we homeschool."

At that moment, my husband and I locked eyes — and it hit us:
This is the good stuff.
This is what we had been missing.

The freedom to say yes to spontaneous fun.
The freedom to live fully, without fear of being late, behind, or boxed in.

Because in homeschooling...
There's always tomorrow.

Planning Without Panic: Building Your Framework

Now that you're breathing again, let's talk about how to actually create a homeschool flow that works for you — without tears, spreadsheets, or caffeine overdoses.

When you're sketching out your year, your month, or even just your week, think about your framework first:

→ What subjects or skills does my child need to learn?

→ How can we fit that into our real life — not the fantasy one I wish I had?

→ How can I leave space for life to happen?

That's it.
That's the whole secret.

Framework Step 1: What Subjects or Skills Does My Child Need to Learn?

Start here.
Not with Pinterest.
Not with the neighbor's color-coded master list.
Not with the "Top 50 Homeschool Must-Haves" blog post that somehow made you feel like you're already failing.

Ask yourself:

- What math do they need this year?
- What level of reading, writing, and spelling?
- What history or science topics are we exploring?
- What habits of faith and character are we building through Bible study?

Some subjects will naturally weave together.
(Especially if you're using a classical model where topics layer and connect across subjects.)
Others will stand alone.

Either way, don't feel like you have to tackle every single subject every single day. Big picture goals matter more than daily checkboxes.

> You're not trying to "cover it all."
> You're laying strong foundations for thinking, living, and loving to learn.

Older kids?
Check your state's graduation requirements and write down what's really needed.
(Only what's required — not what random Internet strangers are yelling about.)

Quick Note: What the Heck *Is* Classical Education?

I've mentioned it a couple of times now, and you may be asking yourself, "What the heck even is that?"

Fair question.

When I say "classical," I'm not talking about togas and scrolls.
Classical education is an approach that focuses on teaching kids *how* to think—not just what to think—using a three-part model called the trivium: Grammar (knowledge), Logic (understanding), and Rhetoric (wisdom and communication).

It leans on great books, big questions, and timeless truths.
Basically: less test prep, more truth-seeking.
And yes… sometimes Latin. But don't panic—we ditched it for Spanish and nobody called the classical police.

Framework Step 2: How Can We Fit It Into Our Real Life?

Homeschooling isn't about wedging your family into a fake, rigid routine that somebody else made up.

It's about asking:

- Are we morning people or slow-start people? (*We don't rise and shine. We rise and... eventually function.*)
- Are there co-ops, sports, livestock shows, or real-life commitments we need to schedule around?
- Are Mondays a lost cause? (No judgment.)
- Do we need a lighter load some days because of work or family stuff?

In our house, Mondays are basically spoken for.
We're part of a homeschool group that takes up our entire day.
Schoolwork still happens, but the day is full and busy, and we know better than to plan anything else on top of it.

And from January to April?
Welcome to show season.

This past year, we packed in seven fairs in just six weeks — and that wasn't even all of them.
That was just one particularly wild stretch.

We live in Florida, but we travel all over the state... and sometimes even haul to Louisiana, Texas, and beyond.

Some days, we knock out a few assignments here and there at a show.
Other days, the books stay closed — and the boots stay on.

And you know what?
That's OK.

We catch up later — during slower weeks, late spring, summer afternoons when life isn't so crazy.

And let's be honest:
They're learning just as much in the barn and the show ring as they would be sitting at a desk.

- Responsibility.
- Hard work.
- Commitment.
- Problem-solving.
- Grace under pressure.

Those lessons don't always come from a workbook — and that's part of the beauty of homeschooling, too.

You can stack subjects.
That means combining multiple subjects into one lesson or activity. Reading historical fiction? You're hitting history *and* literature. Doing a science experiment and writing about it? Boom—science, writing, and critical thinking all in one.

> Flexibility isn't failure.
> Flexibility is a feature.

You can loop them.
Instead of sticking to

a rigid daily schedule, loop scheduling lets you rotate through subjects. You work through your list one at a time, and when you finish, you loop back to the top. No guilt if something gets skipped—just pick up where you left off.

You can double up when energy is high and take breaks when life demands it.

Framework Step 3: How Can I Leave Space for Life to Happen?

I can plan for the things I know are coming —
the homeschool group days that fill our Mondays,
the fairs and livestock shows that keep us traveling
and busy for weeks at a time.

But what about the stuff that pops up out of nowhere?

This is the magic nobody talks about enough.

Life will interrupt your perfect plans.

- Sick days will happen.
- Appointments will appear.
- The tire will blow.
- The dog will throw up on the math book.
- Some mornings, your kid will just need an extra hug and an extra hour before they can find their math brain.

Plan for it.

Build margin into your days and weeks.
Leave room for catch-up days, field trips, random museum visits, pajama mornings, and spontaneous lessons that don't come from a book.

Margin isn't a backup plan.
Margin is the plan.

And believe me — I thought I understood this after five years of homeschooling.
I thought I had finally figured out the right balance between planning and flexibility.

But this past year?
God reminded me just how important margin really is.

In November, I had an unexpected hysterectomy.
And because life never asks if it's a good time, I ended up with an infection that made recovery a whole lot harder.

My mom, who was helping care for me (because my amazing husband was working through his busiest season), broke her foot.
And yes, as an only child, I was supposed to be taking care of her!
Thank God for amazing mother-in-laws and friends who stepped in when we couldn't.

A few days after Christmas, we lost our family dog —
right in the middle of what should have been a season
of celebrating and resting.

Then, I spent a week in the hospital, clinging to family
as we hurdled toward the devastating loss of a loved
one.

The following week was a blur of grief, togetherness,
and just... surviving.

All of this... in the span of seven weeks.

School?
What even was school?

We picked up pieces when we could.
We rested when we needed to.
We grieved.
We leaned on the flexibility we had built into our lives
— and we survived.

That's why margin matters.

You can plan your days beautifully, but life is still going
to write its own surprises into the margins.

Plan Your Homeschool Year Like You're Taking a Long Road Trip

You don't fill the schedule bumper to bumper —
you leave space for unexpected detours, snack breaks, wrong turns, and all the little moments that make the journey memorable.

What Works for Us (And Why That's All That Matters)

Here's a little example of what *actually* works in our house—and I say this knowing it won't be found in any boxed curriculum planner.

We only do math from **April to August**.
That's right.
Just math.
Just those months.

We might sprinkle in a little during the rest of the year if we feel like it, but our main math season is spring and summer. And let me be clear—math is *the bane* of my existence. My kids are okay at it. Nobody's sobbing over long division. But nobody's thrilled either. (Except my husband. He's basically Rain Man. He doesn't even *need* a calculator. It's borderline unfair.)

For a while, math was wrecking our days.
It stole the joy.
We'd finish a lesson and feel like we'd run a marathon,

only to realize we still had spelling, history, and science waiting in the wings.
Some days were fine.
Most were just... heavy.

So one year, I put it down.
Not forever.
Just until our long Thanksgiving-to-New-Year break.

No new group assignments were rolling in, and I figured we'd just rest and reset.
But then I had an idea:
What if we only focused on math — no other subjects, no distractions, just math and a little quiet reading time?

And guess what?

My kids took off.
Without the mental clutter of everything else, they actually *focused*. They remembered what we did yesterday. They made progress. And they didn't hate it.

So now?
That's how we do it.
April to August = math season.
Fall and winter =

> You don't need a schedule that impresses strangers. You need one that serves your family.

everything else (plus livestock shows, holidays, and hanging on by a thread some days).

It's not traditional.
It's not textbook.
But it's *ours*.
And it works.

So if math on Tuesdays and grammar in the bathtub makes your life smoother?
Do it.
Call it school.
And move on.

That's the freedom you signed up for.
Use it.

CHAPTER 7:

Groups, Co-Ops, and Socialization

AKA, "Will My Kid Have Friends?"

Ah, yes.
Socialization.
That word people love to whisper about like it's code for:
"*Are you ruining your children?*"

I always find it funny that the very first thing people ask about homeschooling isn't,
"*What curriculum are you using?*"
or
"*Are you surviving math?*"

Nope.
Straight to:
"*But what about friends?*"

Here's the thing:
I went to regular school.

I taught in regular school.
You know, what a lot of school actually teaches you about socialization?

How to sit still, be quiet, and not talk to the people next to you.

(Disclaimer: I know a ton of amazing kids who are thriving in public and private schools — and this is absolutely not a knock on them.)

> Maybe — just maybe — we can stop assuming homeschooled kids are destined to become unsocialized hermits.

But just like I don't ask public or private school parents if their kids are going to be weird or different because of their schooling choice...

Finding Community

As I mentioned earlier, we are part of a homeschool group — and it has been such a gift.

For a while, we were simply members of a group we loved. We loved it so much that over time, God began to steer our hearts toward something new — something different.

Doors started opening.
Conversations happened.

A friend and I found ourselves feeling strong convictions about starting a group with certain elements we couldn't find anywhere around us.

It wasn't something we rushed into lightly.
It took a lot of prayer, a lot of late-night talks, and eventually... a lot of blood, sweat, and so. many. tears.

But it has been so worth it.

The community that's grown out of that leap of faith has become more than a homeschool group —
it's become a family.

And honestly?
I couldn't imagine doing this homeschool life without them now.

Finding Freedom

However (and this is huge) — this is what works for our family.
It doesn't mean it's the best thing for everyone.
It doesn't mean it's a required step to "homeschool success."

Some families thrive in groups.
Some thrive in the quiet and solitude of home.
Some families love groups — but end up in completely different groups than their friends because God has different places for them to grow.

And that's okay.

One family might need lots of activities, sports, and field trips.
Another family might need slower rhythms, backyard science experiments, and margin to breathe deeply.

Both are homeschooling "the right way" — because both are homeschooling in a way that fits their unique family.

Community is a blessing — but so is the freedom to walk your own path.

You don't have to "fix" a situation that's working beautifully just because it looks different than your neighbor's.
And you don't have to defend a quieter season if that's what your family needs most right now.

Homeschooling isn't about fitting a mold.
It's about finding what makes your family thrive.

And sometimes...
Thriving looks different than you thought it would.

If You Want Community: Finding Your People

If you're craving community — whether it's for your kids, for yourself, or for both — there are more options than ever before.
But a little real talk before we dive in:

You probably won't find the perfect group.

Trust me — ours is amazing, but even we are just a bunch of imperfect people doing our best and eating way too many snacks.

Most groups will have quirks, flaws, awkward moments, and the occasional potluck incident you pretend never happened.

That's normal.

Here's where to start:

> You're not looking for perfection — you're looking for your people.

1. Check Out Local Homeschool Groups

   - Facebook homeschool groups (yes, they're still a thing)
   - Church-based co-ops or enrichment programs
   - Field trip groups
   - Park day meetups
   - Special-interest groups (like STEM clubs, nature groups, or book clubs)

Don't be afraid to visit a few and "date around" before you commit.

2. Start Small

You don't have to sign up for an entire curriculum package, weekly co-op, and three sports leagues tomorrow.
Start with one event.
One park day.
One field trip.
See how it feels — and trust your gut.

3. Be Patient

It can take time to find a community.
It can feel awkward at first.
Like middle school cafeteria awkward. That doesn't mean you're doing it wrong — it just means you're human.

Friendships — real ones — take time to grow.
Give it time. Stay open. Stay kind. Stay real.

4. If You Can't Find It... Maybe You're Being Called to Build It

(Ask me how I know. 😅)

If your area doesn't have the kind of group you're looking for,
maybe you're the one God's nudging to start it.

Even if it's just inviting two other families to a park once a month.

Big things often start small.

(And yes... it might involve blood, sweat, and tears.
But it might also build a family.)

If You Don't Want (or Can't Find) Community: Thriving Anyway

Maybe you're in a season where group life just doesn't fit.
Maybe your kids are little.
Maybe your family is healing from a hard season.
Maybe you looked around and said, "Nope. Not for us right now."

That's not just okay — it can be a huge blessing.

Here's how to thrive without feeling like you're "missing" something:

1. Find Small, Intentional Connections

It doesn't have to be a giant group.

- One solid friend.
- One family to meet at the park once a month.
- One cousin, one neighbor, one pen pal across the country.

Small is still socialization.
Small is still beautiful.

2. Embrace the Season

Some seasons are about building community.
Some are about building your home.
Some are about deepening your family bonds without a million outside voices.

God uses both.
Don't rush what He's doing in your quiet seasons.

3. Socialization Happens in Real Life Too

- Running errands.
- Serving at church.
- Hanging out with grandparents.
- Meeting neighbors.
- Talking with people at the feed store or the post office.

Socialization isn't an event.
It's life lived alongside people.

And homeschooling gives you the gift of doing that in a deeper, richer way than a thirty-minute lunch break between bells.

This is Socialization

Whether you find a giant group, a tiny circle, or a season of solitude — you're not failing.

You're building something good.
You're building something lasting.
You're building connection... in the way your family needs most.

And if anyone still tries to whisper, "But what about socialization?"
Just smile, nod, and go live your amazing, rich, real life.
(Preferably in pajamas, at the park, while your kids teach a stranger's toddler how to share a ball.)

Comeback Collection

In case you ever need a little extra boost when someone tilts their head and whispers,
"But what about socialization?" —
here are a few ready-to-go answers you can use with a smile (or at least a polite smirk):

- "Don't worry — they're plenty socialized. In fact, sometimes they're a little too socialized. You want 'em for a few hours?"

- "We actually had a meeting about that with our principal, guidance counselor, cafeteria lady, and PE coach. (It was me.) We all agreed it's going great."

- "I'd be more worried if they weren't a little weird. Normal is overrated."

- "They've got friends. And siblings. And chickens. Honestly, some days the chickens are better company."
- "They know how to be kind, brave, and interesting. We'll call that a win."
- "If by socialization, you mean 'learning how to share snacks, argue over Monopoly, and form backyard alliances,' we're thriving."

> you don't owe anyone a PowerPoint presentation explaining why your kid will be just fine.

At the end of the day,

Smile. Nod. Maybe toss out a witty one-liner. And then go back to living your best (slightly messy, pajama-clad) homeschool life.

CHAPTER 8:

The Beauty of Pajama Days

*Learning Doesn't Always Look Like
Pen and Paper*

Some of the very best homeschool days don't look anything like "school" at all.

Some of the best days start in pajamas...
and stay that way.

And let's be honest — some of the worst days start with everyone fully dressed at 8 a.m., color-coded schedules proudly displayed, and tears by 10:07.

The truth is:
Real learning doesn't have to look like a desk, a worksheet, and a sharpened pencil.

> Learning happens when you least expect it — when life, curiosity, and connection collide.

And honestly?
That's where the magic is.

Learning Happens Everywhere

You don't have to chase perfection to chase real education.

- Cooking dinner together can be math, science, reading comprehension, and life skills — all in one messy, delicious afternoon.
- Watching a documentary can be your history lesson for the day. (Bonus points if you pause halfway through and debate conspiracy theories over popcorn.)
- A good math board game can replace the workbook — and sometimes teach critical thinking even better.
- Folding laundry while listening to an audiobook can turn into an entire literature study, complete with laughter and sock wars.
- Playing outside and measuring how far you can throw a rock? That's physics.
- Building a Lego castle? Architecture and engineering.
- Arguing over who fed the chickens? Debate team training. (And conflict resolution practice.)

Learning is happening all the time —
whether there's a worksheet involved or not.

Mrs. Frizzle Was Onto Something

You know who really understood what learning could look like?
Mrs. Frizzle.

The Magic School Bus wasn't just a cartoon.
It was a masterclass in how real education works:

- Field trips.
- Experiments.
- Wild guesses.
- Getting messy.
- Making mistakes.
- Asking big questions.

Actually living the learning instead of just memorizing it for a quiz.

Mrs. Frizzle didn't hand out worksheets and sit quietly at her desk.
She grabbed a sparkly dress, hopped into a psychedelic bus, and took her kids into the subject.

No one stayed clean.
No one stayed bored.
Everyone learned something.

And if you needed permission to declare that watching *The Magic School Bus* totally counts as science class?

Consider it officially granted.
(*Seatbelts, everyone!*)

Why This Matters

You're not "falling behind" because you swapped math worksheets for a game day.

You're not "failing" because you taught history through a documentary and some passionate dinner conversation.

You're not "doing it wrong" if your science lesson happened with baking soda, vinegar, and a backyard volcano instead of a bubble test.

You're not "cheating" because your kid learned fractions by doubling a cookie recipe.

You're raising:

- Thinkers.
- Problem-solvers.
- Communicators.
- Innovators.

Humans who know how to connect, question, build, and create.

And that's a whole lot more valuable than a stack of perfectly completed worksheets tucked in a drawer somewhere.

Real Learning, Real Life: My "No More Cooking" Story

I've talked about how we're part of a growing homeschool group.
Well — it's growing fast.

We write the curriculum, organize everything, teach upper grades, and (thankfully) have some incredible parents who help carry the load.

But this past season?
Life got crazy.
Planning for the upcoming year felt like drinking from a fire hose, and honestly?

I was tired — still grieving a hard season, still catching my breath, and still trying to find my footing in the middle of it all.

In my exhaustion — and maybe a tiny bit of desperation — I made a bold executive decision:

I was officially retiring from cooking on Tuesdays and Thursdays.

My kids, who are 12 and 13, were now in charge.
(YIKES. I know.)

Honestly, I fully expected frozen pizzas and bagged salad kits to show up on the table.
Maybe some sandwiches if they were feeling fancy.

But y'all.
I have been blown away.

We're talking:

- Cheeseburger sliders with homemade tater tots (Did you even know you can make those?! Because I sure didn't!)
- Beer-battered fish and chips from scratch (It was a literal miracle the house didn't burn down with the amount of oil dangerously close to the gas flame... but we're all here, a little wiser, a little greasier, and a whole lot more cautious now.)
- Grilled chicken and fresh sautéed vegetables
- Thoughtful meals planned, prepped, and executed — with pride.

They find the recipes.
They make a grocery list.
They cook the meal start to finish — with exactly zero help from me.

And when they do come asking for help, I just smile and ask,
"Where could you go to find that out?"

They've learned:

- Research skills

- Planning and preparation
- Grocery budgeting
- Cooking technique
- Time management
- Teamwork
- Safety (*lots* of safety)

And honestly?
They've taken more ownership and pride in the kitchen than I ever imagined.

They eagerly look forward to their cooking nights now —
and, if I'm being completely honest, so do we.
Fewer dishes for me. Better dinners for everyone.
Win-win.

Real learning sneaks up on you sometimes.

It doesn't always come from a workbook or a carefully planned curriculum.
Sometimes, it walks into your kitchen with a sack of potatoes, a stubborn streak, and a YouTube video on "how to make homemade tater tots."

> Learning found us... even in the middle of exhaustion.

And it's beautiful.

Give Yourself Permission

Give yourself — and your kids — permission to:

- Learn in the kitchen.
- Learn in the yard.
- Learn in the car.
- Learn on the couch in pajamas at 2 p.m. with a documentary and a plate of cookies.
- Learn without panic when the schedule falls apart.
- Learn in loud, messy, beautiful ways that don't fit neat little boxes.

And people don't learn best in boxes.
They learn best through wonder, movement, questions, and real connection.

The beauty of homeschooling isn't just found in lesson plans or finished workbooks.
It's found in the life you're building —
one pajama-clad, cookie-eating, backyard-experiment kind of day at a time.

It's in the messy kitchen.
It's in the late-night questions.
It's in the unexpected field trips and the conversations that wander into places no textbook could have predicted.

Real learning is everywhere.

You don't have to chase checklists.
You just have to keep chasing wonder.

> You're not just raising students.
> You're raising people.

Part III:

Handling the Hard Stuff

CHAPTER 9:

When It's Hard (Because It Will Be)

Slowing Down, Speeding Up, and Staying Sane

Before we dive in, let's just rip off the Band-Aid:

Homeschooling is beautiful.
Homeschooling is rewarding.
Homeschooling is one of the best decisions we have ever made.

And homeschooling will absolutely, 100% kick your tail some days.

That doesn't mean you're failing.
It just means you're doing it for real.

Some days, you'll feel like Wonder Woman in a messy bun—

taming chaos, sparking joy, and throwing spontaneous science experiments into the schedule like a boss.

Other days, you'll seriously consider enrolling everyone in boarding school by lunchtime.
(And yes, Googling it while crying into your Dr Pepper totally counts as multitasking.)

It's all part of the story.

Up until now, we've talked a lot about practical things:

- Slowing down
- Speeding up
- Building margin
- Flexibility over perfection

And those things matter — a lot.

But now?
We're not just talking about how to plan for hard days.

We're talking about how to survive them
— emotionally.

Because when the wheels fall off, it's not just your schedule that takes a hit.
It's your heart.
It's your confidence.

It's your mind playing tricks on you, whispering,
"You're failing. You're ruining everything."

This chapter isn't about fixing your planner.
It's about finding grace.
It's about emotional survival.
It's about what to do when homeschooling feels like it's crushing you instead of blessing you.

And if you're there
— or when you get there —
you're not broken.
You're not a bad mom.
You're not a bad teacher.
You're just...human.

> Hard days aren't the end of your story. They're the messy middle where the real growth happens.

When It's Hard, Remember:

1. You Can Slow Down

If the day is melting down around you...
slow it down.

You don't have to barrel forward because the checklist says so.
You don't have to cram another math lesson into a brain that's clearly full.

One of the best gifts of homeschooling is that you control the pace — not the clock.

Slow learning isn't bad learning.
Sometimes, slowing down is exactly what real growth looks like.

2. You Can Speed Up

If your kid is flying through a concept?
If something clicks like magic?

Speed it up!

You don't have to drag a lesson out for six weeks just because someone else's pacing guide says you should.

Mastery matters more than mileage.

If they get it, move on.
If they're thriving, let them run.

Flexibility isn't failing — it's flourishing.

3. You Are Allowed to Pivot

(If you just said "pivot, pivot, pivot" followed by "shutup, shutup, shutup"...you are my people.😂)

Sometimes the thing you thought would work... doesn't.

Sometimes the curriculum you loved online turns out to be about as fun as watching paint dry.
Sometimes the perfect schedule you spent hours planning...crashes and burns before breakfast.

Pivot anyway.

Switch it up.
Tweak it.
Take a break.
Start fresh.

> You are not failing when you change course. You're being wise.

Pivoting isn't quitting.
It's adapting — and adapting is one of the greatest life skills you can model for your kids.

And sometimes?
Pivoting looks like making popcorn and calling it a read-aloud snack break.
Or turning on an audiobook while you all sprawl on the floor.
It's screen time. (*Yes, it is* OK.)
It's piling in the car for a drive and an ice-cold, crisp Dr. Pepper that tastes like a survival medal.
It's kicking the kids outside and letting the sun do some of the work.

Whatever it takes — **pivot with peace**.
You've got permission.

Real Life Story: That Time I Threw a Math Book

In case you think I'm preaching this from some mountaintop of wisdom and patience…let me tell you about the day I completely lost it over math.

My son who, bless him, inherited my math brain — which is to say, it's more of a math suggestion than a math brain, was working on plotting points.

Plotting points, y'all.
Just simple graphing.

And every single time we hit zero, he moved.
Every. Single. Time.

I explained it every way I knew how.
I used drawings, songs, examples, interpretive dance — you name it.

Finally, desperate, I had him stand up.

"Okay. Now take ZERO steps."
I said it slowly. Clearly.

And guess what he did?

Yep.
He moved.

Y'all.
I melted.
I snapped.

In what can only be described as an Olympic-level tantrum, I shouted,
"MATH IS OVER!"
and threw the math book across the room.

I'm not proud of it.
(Okay, maybe a tiny bit proud of the distance I got with that book. 🏆)

But mostly?
I felt like a complete failure.

As a teacher.
As a mom.
As a human.

I had to cool down.
I had to apologize.
I had to own the fact that my frustration wasn't his fault.

And then...we started over.
We found some videos.
We made it fun.

We built back trust — and math skills — together.

I failed in the moment.
But I wasn't a failure.

There's a difference.
And learning that difference changed everything.

Faithfulness Over Flawlessness

Homeschooling isn't supposed to be easy every day.
It's supposed to be worth it every day.

This is exactly when you reach for the "why" you wrote down — because feelings lie, but purpose doesn't.

You're going to have days when you doubt yourself.
You're going to have moments when you want to quit.

That doesn't make you weak.
It makes you real.
And real is where the best parts of life happen.

> The beauty isn't in having easy days.
> The beauty is in showing up on the hard ones.

Some days, homeschooling will feel like climbing a mountain barefoot, carrying a goat, in the rain. Other days, it'll feel like dancing through fields of daisies.

Most days?
It's a little bit of both.

When it's Hard:

- Breathe.
- Slow down if you need to.
- Speed up if you can.
- Pivot without guilt.
- Laugh when you can.
- Cry when you need to.
- Pray without ceasing.

You're not just homeschooling through books.
You're homeschooling through real life —
through grief, through meltdowns, through triumphs,
through tattered schedules and unexpected miracles.

And some days?

You'll throw a math book across the room,
pick it back up (or leave it where you threw it — no judgment),
apologize,
and try again.

And that matters too.

Because the best part?

God doesn't grade you on how smooth
the journey looks.
He's grading you on faithfulness.

And faithful doesn't always look pretty.
It just keeps showing up.

You've got this.
And when you don't? He does.

CHAPTER 10:
Testing, Grading, and Other Things You Don't Have to Fear

Keeping Track Without Losing Sight

Some kids ace tests.
Some kids ace life.
Know which one matters more.

If the words *"testing"* and *"grading"* send a shiver down your spine —
breathe.

You're not about to be shackled to a Scantron machine.
You're not doomed to a life of red pens, tears, and self-doubt.

Testing and grading are tools — not tyrants.
They're supposed to serve your homeschool life, not steal your joy.

And if you use them wisely, they can actually be a blessing.

- ✅ They can show you what's sticking.
- ✅ They can reveal where more practice is needed.
- ✅ They can teach kids how to work hard, aim high, and handle feedback with grace.

But here's the most important thing to remember:

Every Milestone Looks Different

Some kids ace tests as if it's their superpower.
Some kids bomb every test but could out-discuss, out-think, and out-analyze everyone else in the room.

> Testing is a snapshot.
> It is not the whole story.

And if we're being honest, which one sounds more like actual learning to you?

There's a famous quote — nobody knows exactly who said it first, but it's brilliant:

"Everybody is a genius. But if you judge a fish by its ability to climb a tree, it will live its whole life believing that it is stupid."

That's testing, in a nutshell.

Tests measure *some* things.
They do not measure everything that matters.

What We Do (and Why)

At Apex, our homeschool group, we do give quizzes, tests, and even final exams for our upper-grade students.

But here's the key:
We don't grade them. Parents do.

Parents grade their child's work and have complete freedom to:

- Allow redos
- Adjust scores
- Use test results as feedback — not final judgment

We believe it's good and healthy for kids to be pushed, challenged, and held to real expectations.
(Hello, real life!)

BUT we also believe tests aren't the final word.
They're just one tool to help you see where growth is happening — and where extra support might be needed.

Grading Without Losing Your Mind

Testing is one thing.
Grading is another.

And if the word *"grading"* makes you want to break out in hives...
you are not alone.

One of the most common questions I hear from new homeschool parents is:
"How do I even grade their work?"

Here's the simple truth:

You get to decide what grading looks like for your homeschool.

There's no universal homeschool grading fairy floating around, slapping A's and B's on your kitchen table work. (Although...side hustle idea?)

You have freedom — and responsibility — to create a grading system that fits:

- Your child's learning style
- Your family's goals
- Your state's legal requirements (if there are any)

✅ Some families use traditional percentages and letter grades.

- ✅ Some use a "Complete/Incomplete" approach.
- ✅ Some focus on mastery — allowing kids to redo work until it's understood instead of handing out low grades.
- ✅ Some use project rubrics, discussion points, or presentation evaluations.

There's no one right way to do it.

At Apex, we send home the work, but it's parents who hold the pen (and the final call).
Some grade strictly.
Some allow for corrections and growth.
Some simply focus on whether mastery is happening over time.

And honestly?

A grade is a tool, not a tattoo.
It's not a life sentence.
It's just information.

Practical Tips for Grading at Home:

- Focus on Progress Over Perfection
  Is your child growing? Stretching? Learning?
  That's what matters most.

- Grade the Process, Not Just the Product
  Effort, perseverance, creativity — all of it counts.

- Use Mistakes as Launchpads, Not Labels
  Mistakes aren't the enemy. They're the fastest path to deeper understanding.

- Be Honest, But Be Kind
  Yes, hold your kids to standards.
  But remember: they're whole humans, not just a math score or a spelling test.

- Adjust Your Expectations Over Time
  A second grader's "A" looks different than a high school junior's "A."
  And that's exactly how it should be.

Quick Note:

Every state has its own homeschool laws — including what's required (or not) when it comes to grades, transcripts, and documentation. Be sure to look up the homeschool statutes for *your* state so you can stay on track legally while doing what works best for your family.

When Tests Don't Tell the Whole Story

If your child bombs a test?
First of all — breathe.

It doesn't mean they're lazy.
It doesn't mean you're a failure.
It doesn't mean they're doomed to live in your basement, eating frozen pizza at 35.

It just means it's time to dig a little deeper:

- Did they not grasp the material?
- Were they stressed and panicked?
- Was the test format a poor fit for their learning style?
- Could they show their knowledge in a different way?
- If they truly don't understand it — slow down.
  Find new ways to teach it.
  Use videos, games, projects, conversation — whatever clicks.

If they do understand but test poorly — mix in other ways to assess them:

- Oral presentations
- Projects
- One-on-one discussions
- Creative writing
- Teaching it back to you
- There are a hundred ways to show mastery.
  And many of them don't involve a bubble sheet.

What Actually Matters

Use tests if they help you.
Give grades if they help your child stretch and grow.

But don't lose sight of the bigger picture.

You're not raising perfect test-takers.
You're raising:

- Thinkers
- Problem-solvers
- Leaders
- Dreamers
- Workers
- Creators
- Sometimes they'll ace the test.
  Sometimes they'll ace life — and the test won't even know what hit it.

And that's the kind of education worth fighting for.

CHAPTER 11:

Transcripts, High School Credits, and Graduation

You're Not Too Late to Do This

Let's be honest:
The words "transcripts" and "high school credits" sound terrifying — like you need a three-ring binder, a fancy seal, and an extra degree in guidance counseling just to figure them out.

And "graduation"?
That sounds like something only *real* schools do — you know, the ones with yearbooks, valedictorians, and snack bar nachos that cost $7.

But here's the good news:
You can 100% homeschool high school successfully — without a professional printer, without a principal's office, and definitely without having a panic attack.

You are not too late.
You are not underqualified.
You are not going to ruin your kid's future because you didn't think about this when they were in second grade.

If your child is anywhere between "barely starting 9th grade" and "oh no, we're halfway through junior year and I haven't even thought about credits" — you're still fine.

And if you're thinking about transcripts while they're still wearing Minecraft pajamas and losing teeth? Congratulations. You're basically a homeschool valedictorian already.

In this chapter, I'm going to break it down into normal-people language.
Not school district language.
Not corporate-education-jargon language.
Just real talk about what you actually need to know — and how to do it without losing your mind.

Spoiler:
You're probably already doing better than you think.

What Is a Transcript (Really)?

A transcript is just a list.
That's it.

It's a clean, organized sheet of paper that says:

- Here's what my student studied.
- Here's what year they studied it.
- Here's the grade they earned.
- It's not a magic document.

It's not a secret government file.
It's not something you have to hire an expert to create for you (unless you just really love paying other people for stuff you can totally do yourself).

The truth is:

Most transcripts have the same basic parts:

> If you can make a grocery list, you can make a transcript.

- Student's name
- School Name (Yes, you get to name your homeschool — and it instantly sounds official! Some states require you to list a school name for records, while others leave it optional.)
- Course titles
- Years/semesters completed
- Grades earned
- Total credits earned

- GPA (optional but helpful)
- Graduation date
- That's it.

No embossed gold seal necessary.
Unless you want to get fancy — then, by all means, go full Hogwarts.

A Note About Course Codes (Optional, but Helpful)

Some colleges like to see course codes on transcripts. It's not required, but adding them can make your transcript look a little more official and easier for admission offices to review.

In my state (Florida), the Department of Education publishes a course code list every year.
I just find the course that matches what my kids took and jot down the code next to the class title. Simple and done.

When Should You Start a Transcript?

Ideally?
When your child starts 9th grade (or whenever you officially start counting high school-level work).

But if you're late starting and your kid is halfway through high school?
Take a deep breath.

You can absolutely go back and fill in the details based on what they've already done.

You might have to dig through some old planners, text messages to yourself, or mental notes like,
"Oh yeah, 10th grade was the year we accidentally turned field trips into a full Geography credit."

It's doable.
Promise.

For the record?
My kids' transcripts right now are literally living in a Google Doc that I pray doesn't get accidentally deleted. (Real life, friends.)

You don't have to have it all polished and printed in 9th grade.
You just need a place to track it.

Also — yes — I'm keeping transcripts already for my 6th and 7th graders, because they're taking some high school–level courses.

It's totally OK to start tracking early if your child is ready.
You're not boxed in by traditional grade levels anymore.

Remember:
In public school, Geometry has traditionally been a 10th-grade class...
but it doesn't have to fit in that box anymore.

If your 7th grader is crushing Algebra, or your 8th grader knocks out Biology — go ahead and record it! It counts.

How Do You Track High School Credits?

Here's the quick rule of thumb most homeschoolers follow:

If They Complete...	It Counts As...
A full-year course (around 120–180 hours)	1 full credit
A semester-long course (around 60–90 hours)	0.5 credit

(Note: *These aren't laws. They're flexible guidelines used by schools and colleges. You can adjust hours a little if needed.*)

You're basically aiming to show:

- My kid studied Algebra for a full year = 1 credit.
- My kid studied Personal Finance for one semester = 0.5 credit.
- You're building a story about their education — one course and one credit at a time.

What Classes Count for Credit?

Short answer:
Way more than you think.

Of course, the basics count:

- English (literature, composition, grammar, etc.)
- Math (Algebra, Geometry, etc.)
- Science (with or without labs — think Biology, Chemistry, Physics)
- History/Social Studies (World History, U.S. History, Government, Economics)
- But electives and creative classes count too:
- Art, Music, Theater
- Computer Science
- Business or Entrepreneurship
- Life Skills
- Physical Education (yes, even if it's running around the backyard)
- Foreign Language (even if it's Duolingo plus practice)

Pro Tip:

Colleges aren't expecting a super rigid, cookie-cutter transcript from homeschoolers.

They actually like seeing electives, personal interests, and unique courses that show depth and creativity.

Your kid's love for robotics, culinary arts, or photography can absolutely be part of their official high school story.

Graduation: Yes, You Can Actually Hand Them a Diploma

You — the parent — have the legal right to graduate your child and issue their diploma.

(Go ahead. Let that sink in. It's that simple.)

You don't have to:

- Hire a lawyer
- Apply to the State Department of Education
- Beg an accredited academy to bless you

You decide when your child has met your graduation standards.***

You issue their diploma.
You celebrate with every ounce of joy, relief, and ugly crying you have left.

Optional Diploma Ideas:

- Order a nice printed diploma online (tons of sites make them look amazing for $30–$50)
- Create your own with a beautiful template and a little Canva magic
- Host a small ceremony with family, friends, or your homeschool group

Fun fact:
Many colleges, military branches, and employers have accepted parent-issued diplomas for decades.

***Quick Disclaimer:

While you have a lot of freedom to build your homeschool transcript, you still need to make sure your student meets your state's graduation requirements — and the requirements of whatever college, trade school, or program they're aiming for.

> Homeschoolers have been quietly out here graduating real humans all along.

Almost every university has a section on their admissions website specifically for homeschoolers. (Look for it — it's usually under "Freshman Admissions" or "Homeschool Applicants.")
They'll tell you exactly what they expect — and sometimes it's a little different from what's required for traditional high schoolers.

Don't be afraid to call or even set up a meeting in person.

Admissions offices are usually happy to walk you through what they want to see. It shows that you're serious — and it can save you a lot of guesswork and stress later.

Also, be aware that some programs want more than your state's minimum requirements.

For example:

- In Florida, students technically only need 24 credits to graduate from high school.
- But Florida State University (FSU) states that the average accepted freshman has completed over 30 high school credits — far more than the minimum.

Moral of the story?
You're in charge, but don't leave anything important out.

Think of it like packing for a trip:
You get to pick your suitcase, but you still need to make sure you bring the right stuff if you want to get where you're going.

What If You Mess It Up?

Here's the truth nobody tells you:

Even traditional schools sometimes mess up transcripts.
(Shocking, I know.)

If you realize you forgot a class?
- ✅ Add it.

If you realize you miscalculated a credit?
- ✅ Fix it.

Transcripts are living documents until your kid actually sends them off to a college or employer.

You're allowed to update, correct, adjust, and improve as you go.

No one expects perfection — just honesty and effort.

SATs, ACTs, and Other Alphabet Soup

For a long time, the SAT and ACT were considered the golden tickets to college admission.

And while they're still important for some schools and scholarships, they're not always required anymore.

A lot of colleges today are test-optional — meaning your student can choose whether or not to send in their scores.

Some schools still require them.
Some don't care at all.
Some will only want them if you're applying for merit-based scholarships.

(Translation: You don't have to *panic* about it in 9th grade.)

If your student plans to take the SAT or ACT:

- Check to see what their target colleges expect.
- Take practice tests if possible — there are free ones online.
- Plan ahead — most kids take the SAT or ACT for the first time in late 10th or early 11th grade.
- Remember — it's one piece of the application, not the whole story.

And if standardized testing isn't your student's strong suit?
There are tons of schools that don't require scores at all — or that let you submit a portfolio instead. (Another homeschooler win.)

Dual Enrollment: Shortcut to Glory... or Shortcut to Regret?

Dual enrollment sounds like a dream, right?
Get college credit while you're still in high school.
Save time, save money, and skip a few years of busywork and overpriced textbooks.

And honestly, it can be awesome — for some people.

But before you go signing up for every college class with a pulse, you need to pump the brakes and do a little homework first.

Not every college — and definitely not every scholarship — plays nice with dual enrollment.

- Some sports programs, agriculture programs, and even private scholarships require you to come in as a true freshman.
- Some won't touch you if you show up with college credits already tucked in your back pocket.
- Some will tell you, "We love your ambition... now go to a junior college for two years and we'll talk."

Translation?
If your kid has dreams — Division I sports, ag scholarships, livestock judging teams, marching band scholarships, ROTC, whatever — figure out the rules before you box yourself into a corner.

Don't accidentally build a transcript that looks shiny but secretly slams the door on their dreams.

Dual enrollment can be a rocket ship.
Or it can be a trap door.
It just depends where you're trying to land.

So, before you grab the fast pass, slow down:

- Ask the college.
- Ask the scholarship program.
- Ask the coach.
- Ask your kid about their dreams — even the big, crazy ones.

Because saving six months of tuition isn't worth missing out on the future they were born to build.

CHAPTER 12:

When the Journey Looks Different

Special Needs, Learning Differences, and Homeschooling with Heart

Here's the beautiful truth:
Homeschooling gives kids with special needs or learning differences something they don't always get in traditional classrooms:
A seat at the table without a label.

- No being pulled out of class during the fun stuff.
- No being made to feel "other" because they learn differently.
- No whispering or waiting for special sessions while everyone else moves on.

> At home, your child can just be a student — not a case file.

Their differences can be celebrated, not circled with a red pen.
Their strengths can be amplified, not buried.
Their struggles can be met with compassion, not comparison.

Homeschooling gives you the space to teach the whole child — not just the test scores.

You're Not Alone (And You Don't Have to Invent It All)

The beautiful thing about homeschooling today is that there are more resources than ever for students who learn differently.

You've got access to:

- Specialized curriculums for dyslexia, ADHD, autism, and more
- One-on-one tutoring (in-person or online)
- Speech therapy, occupational therapy, and educational therapy services you can use outside the traditional school system
- Local homeschool groups that are welcoming and inclusive
- Online communities where you can swap ideas, encouragement, and resources

- Flexible learning styles — visual, auditory, hands-on — that you can customize for your child

Need a place to start? Here are a few national resources to explore:

- **SPED Homeschool** – A Christian-led nonprofit providing guidance, curriculum reviews, and community for special education homeschoolers
- **Understood.org** – A secular site with expert-vetted info on learning and thinking differences, including IEP support and parent resources
- **NILD (National Institute for Learning Development)** – Offers educational therapy options and helps parents find trained specialists
- **Wrightslaw** – If you're navigating legal rights or educational evaluations, this site is packed with plain-language info on special education law and advocacy

You don't have to do this alone.
There are communities, tools, and people ready to walk this road with you—faithfully, creatively, and with real hope.

Good news:
You don't have to be an expert.
You just have to be willing to adapt, advocate, and learn alongside your child.

You've already been doing that since the day they were born.
You're more prepared for this than you realize.

Quick Note:

I don't have personal experience homeschooling a student with exceptional learning needs, and I haven't done deep research into every resource listed above. These aren't endorsements — just starting points I've seen recommended often.

What About Diagnoses and IEPs?

If your child already has a diagnosis — autism, dyslexia, ADHD, Down syndrome, sensory processing disorder, or anything else —
that diagnosis doesn't disqualify you from homeschooling.

It empowers you.

Because you already know:

- How your child learns best
- Where they need support
- Where they shine bright

Now you get to tailor their education to fit them — not force them into a system that wasn't designed with their needs in mind.

You can still:

- Work with specialists if needed
- Use therapies that help
- Create goals and track progress
- Celebrate every milestone

You just get to do it on your timeline, not someone else's paperwork deadline.

Some homeschoolers even create an unofficial "learning plan" or "goal sheet" for their own use — no bureaucracy required.

Homeschooling With Differences, Not Around Them

In a homeschool setting:

- Reading struggles don't define your whole day.
- Sensory breaks aren't interruptions — they're part of the plan.
- Hands-on projects can count just as much (if not more!) than traditional tests.
- Your child's gifts — creativity, curiosity, kindness, perseverance — get to take center stage.

Instead of focusing on "fixing" everything, you can focus on growing everything:

- Their confidence
- Their communication
- Their love of learning
- Their belief that they are fearfully and wonderfully made

Because they are.

Instead of Racing a Clock, You Get to Build a Life

In a traditional school, the pressure is constant: *Stay on grade level. Meet the benchmarks. Check the boxes. Keep up.*

At home?

- You can slow down where you need to.
- You can speed up where they thrive.
- You can circle back when something doesn't click the first (or second or third) time.
- You can adjust when life demands it — without apology.

Permission granted:

You can:

- Take a full year (or longer) to master reading fluency if needed.

- Break math lessons into tiny chunks — and celebrate tiny wins.
- Use audiobooks instead of forcing silent reading if that's what keeps the joy alive.
- Let them jump on a trampoline during spelling drills.
- Learn through nature walks, baking days, Lego builds, and science experiments that end with baking soda in your hair.

You don't have to fit into a traditional mold.
You get to build something better.

There's No "One Right Way" — And That's the Best Part

Remember what we talked about earlier?

Homeschooling isn't about recreating someone else's version of success.
It's about building your own.

And when the journey looks different — maybe slower, maybe messier, maybe louder — the same truths still apply:

- Flexibility is a feature, not a flaw.
- Small wins are still wins.
- Progress is more important than perfection.

- Your child's heart matters more than their standardized test scores.

Some families use structured programs.
Some use gentle, child-led learning.
Some use a mix, shifting with the seasons of life.

You get to decide what your homeschool needs to look like.

And you can change your mind at any time without guilt.

Word From My Heart

> Your child is not a problem to fix.
> Your child is a masterpiece to steward.

If you hear nothing else from this chapter, hear this:

Their differences aren't a defect.
They are part of God's design.

Homeschooling lets you:

- Champion their strengths.
- Support their challenges.
- Celebrate their growth — no matter how big or small.

- Walk with them through every high, every low, and every step in between.

You are not failing them by homeschooling.
You are *fighting for them.*

And when you feel tired, overwhelmed, or unsure?
You are *still* exactly who God chose to be their teacher, guide, advocate, and biggest fan.

You're doing holy work.
Even on the hard days.

Especially on the hard days.

CHAPTER 13:

Faith in the Middle

*Why the Messy Middle Matters
More Than You Think*

In Chapter 9, we talked about what to do on the hard days—
the math meltdown days, the messy middle days, the "someone threw a pencil and it wasn't the kid" days.

We discussed slowing down, speeding up, building margin, and choosing flexibility over perfection.

But now?

We need to talk about something deeper.
The days—or seasons—when it's not just a bad day.
It's a *wall*.

- When you start wondering if this whole homeschooling thing was a mistake.

- When you wake up every day, dreading the school part.
- When you look around at your messy house, your messy emotions, and your messy planner and think,
  "*Is this even working?*"
  "*Would they be better off somewhere else?*"
  "*Am I even cut out for this?*"

If that's where you are?

You are not failing.
You are not alone.
And this isn't the end of your story.

What Long-Term Discouragement Looks Like

There's a wall almost every homeschooler hits. Usually sometime in:

- November (the pre-holiday burnout)
- February (the mid-year slump)
- May (the "just cross the finish line" phase)
- It looks like:
- No energy to plan lessons.
- No excitement to start the day.
- Constant second-guessing of your curriculum, your calling, and your own sanity.

- Fantasizing about sending the kids to school and joining a book club where someone else brings the snacks.

Almost every homeschooler goes through it.
It's not a sign you're doing it wrong.
It's a sign you're walking a real road.

What It Doesn't Mean

It doesn't mean:

- You were wrong to start homeschooling.
- You're not "good enough."
- Your kids are doomed.
- God changed His mind about your calling.

It means you're in the middle.

And the middle?
It's where faith grows muscles.

The Middle Is Where the Magic Happens

It's easy to be excited at the beginning.
It's easy to celebrate at the end.

But the middle—
The messy, hard, boring, "is this even working?" middle—

That's where real growth happens.

- It's where Moses wandered with the Israelites for 40 years — after being freed but before reaching the Promised Land.

- It's where David hid from Saul — after being anointed king but before taking the throne.

- It's where Peter sank in the waves — after stepping out of the boat but before reaching Jesus.

You are not stuck.
You are being strengthened.

When It Feels Broken

If you're in a season where the whole thing feels broken, here's what you do:

> The middle is messy because it's where the real transformation happens.

1. Zoom Out

Look back at where you started.
What felt overwhelming then, that feels normal now?
What victories have already happened?
How has your child grown — not just academically, but in character, faith, and life?

Progress doesn't always scream.
Sometimes it whispers.
You have to quiet the chaos long enough to hear it.

And when you do hear it? Celebrate it.
We're quick to get run down by the hard parts, but the wins? We let them flash by like they don't matter.
That spelling word they finally nailed.
The meltdown they worked through.
The prayer they whispered without prompting.

Those are victories.
Don't let them get buried under the noise of what went wrong.
Write them down.
Hang them on the fridge.
Let them shout louder than the moments that tried to steal your joy.

2. Have an Honest Conversation

With yourself.
With God.
With your spouse if you're married.

Ask:

- What's *actually* wearing me down?
- Is it the schedule? The curriculum? The pace?

- Is it a heart issue — mine or theirs?
- Is it fear creeping in again?

Not everything needs to be scrapped.
Sometimes, just a tiny course correction changes everything.

3. Re-evaluate Without Self-Destructing

You're allowed to re-evaluate.
You're allowed to shift gears.

But don't burn the whole thing down just because you had a hard month.

Sometimes you need:

- A lighter load.
- A different curriculum.
- A month of just reading and surviving.
- A nap. (No shame.)

4. Take Quitting Off the Table (Temporarily)

When you hit the wall, promise yourself:

I will not make a major decision while exhausted, overwhelmed, or discouraged.

> Change the "how" without abandoning the "why."

Give it two weeks.

Two weeks of breathing.
Two weeks of adjusting.
Two weeks of lowering the bar and raising the grace.

Then re-evaluate.

Because 99% of the time?

When the exhaustion lifts, so does the panic.

Faith Over Finish Lines

If you're tired, rest.
If you're discouraged, breathe.
If you're doubting, pray.

But don't quit just because the middle feels ugly.

You're not building a perfect transcript.

You're building a life.

You're not planting a flower garden for Instagram.
You're planting a forest that will stand for generations.

And planting?
It's messy.

It's slow.
It's full of dirt and blisters and days when nothing seems to be growing.

But just beneath the surface?
Roots are digging deep.

Roots you can't see yet.

Roots that will hold them strong when the storms come.

The Story Isn't Over

Homeschooling will have:

- Beautiful beginnings
- Ugly middles
- Glorious endings
- And then new beginnings all over again

The middle is not the proof you're failing.
It's the proof you're *in it for the right reasons.*

It's easy to sprint the first mile.
It's easy to sprint across the finish line.

It's the plodding, ordinary, unseen, faithful steps in the middle that define the race.

Keep walking.
Keep planting.
Keep showing up.

God doesn't measure you by how fast you get there.

He measures faithfulness.

And you, my friend, are more faithful than you feel right now.

Part IV:

Bonus Life Lessons They Don't Tell You

CHAPTER 14:

Instagram Lies and Real-Life Wins

*Comparison is the Thief of Joy
(and Sanity)*

Let's just say it straight:
Homeschooling almost never looks like it does on Instagram.

You're going to have days — a lot of them — when it feels like you're the only family not doing morning baskets by candlelight, hand-grinding wheat for homemade bread, crafting color-coded schedules in matching linen jumpsuits, and gracefully diagramming sentences while your children quote C.S. Lewis in Latin.

Meanwhile, you're just trying to find clean socks and hoping everyone brushes their teeth before 2 p.m.

And if you're anything like me, on those days, you'll do the worst thing you can possibly do:

You'll scroll.

Scrolling through:

- Instagram
- Facebook
- Pinterest
- Blogs
- TikTok

Watching all the perfectly curated snapshots of "other" homeschool families.

The ones with:

- Kids smiling while dissecting frogs (no gagging in sight)
- Moms who look camera-ready at 7 a.m.
- Beautiful calligraphy Bible verses hanging over color-coordinated workstations
- Hand-spun, organic, soy candles flickering on reclaimed wood desks
- Nature journals that belong in an art museum

And you'll start thinking:

"Is it just me?"
"Am I failing?"
"Is that what homeschooling is supposed to look like?"

Here's the Truth Nobody Tells You

Maybe their lives *do* look like that.

Maybe they *really* do wake up early and bake sourdough and journal about butterflies before tackling Euclidean geometry in matching bonnets.

Bless them. Truly.

But also?

Maybe it was staged for the photo.

Maybe it's the only clean corner of their house.

Maybe they bribed the kids with marshmallows to smile.

Maybe they cropped out the pile of laundry three feet away.

Or maybe, just maybe, that's the real life God gave them—and it's beautiful.
Just like your real life is beautiful.

Even if it's loud.
Even if it's messy.
Even if today's biggest educational win was explaining how long a hot dog can live on the floor before it becomes a biology experiment.

Start with Heart (Not Aesthetic)

> You don't have to build a picture-perfect homeschool. You have to build a faithful one.

The curated bulletin boards?
The perfect handwriting practice sheets?
The Instagram-worthy nature walks?

Optional.

What matters is:

- A heart that keeps showing up.
- A life where questions are welcomed.
- A home where grace is louder than grammar drills.
- A family that still likes each other at the end of the day (mostly).

Start there.

Everything else is extra frosting.

And honestly? Some days, it's canned frosting straight from the tub. And that's okay, too.

Real Wins > Perfect Pictures

Some of your biggest homeschool victories will never fit inside an Instagram square:

- The day your reluctant reader finishes a chapter without melting down.
- The afternoon when your struggling mathematician finally smiles and says, "Wait...I get it!"
- The messy science experiment that leaves purple dye on the dog's paw for three weeks.
- The dinner table conversation where your kid connects something you taught six months ago and *makes it their own.*
- The moments when you laugh so hard you cry over absolutely nothing...because you were there. Together.

Those are the real wins.

Not polished.
Not perfect.
But so much deeper, so much richer, than any perfectly filtered snapshot.

Another Permission Slip (Because You Probably Need One)

You don't have to homeschool like her.
Or like them.
Or even like the version of yourself you thought you were supposed to be.

You can homeschool like you.

- Messy hair.
- Caffeine-powered brain.
- "Wait, what day is it again?" energy.
- Bravely showing up with whatever you have today.

You were never called to build a Pinterest page.
You were called to build a family.

And you, my friend?

You're doing a lot better than you think.

A Little Real Talk About My "Instagram Days"

> You were never called to perform.
> You were called to be faithful.

We made a cell cake once. I was so proud of the kids — they actually remembered where all the parts went. When it was done, I wanted them to sing the little song they knew and point to the parts on the cake while I filmed it.

The video? Adorable.
The reality? Chaos.

They couldn't get the timing right, someone stuck their finger in the cake mid-song, one had an attitude, and by the time we got a halfway decent take, the whole vibe in the house was wrecked. I *was* proud of them. But if I'm honest—I needed everyone online to see how proud I was too.

Is that a bad thing? Not necessarily.
But when it came at the expense of our joy and peace that day? Yeah... probably.

Gut-Check Questions for When Homeschool Envy Creeps In:

When that comparison game starts playing on repeat in your mind, pause and ask yourself these gut-check questions. Not to shame yourself — but to realign your heart, your calling, and your confidence in the One who called you to this in the first place. Let's get honest

1. **Who am I trying to impress — God or people?**
   Am I wishing for her success because I want the applause, or because I actually want what's best for *my* family? Let's be honest...is this about obedience or ego?

2. **Am I comparing her highlight reel to my behind-the-scenes?**
   God gave *me* these kids, this house, this season, this exact calling. Did I forget that none of it was an accident?

3. **What lie am I swallowing about God or myself?**
   Is the enemy whispering that I'm not enough, or that I need what she has to be worthy, successful, or seen?

4. **Am I being faithful — or just trying to look impressive?**
   God didn't ask me to be Pinterest-perfect. He asked me to be faithful. Am I doing what *He* gave me to do...or am I trying to outshine someone else?

5. **Am I thankful — or just good at grumbling in disguise?**
   When's the last time I noticed the beauty in *my* homeschool instead of nitpicking everything it's not?

6. **What's growing in my heart because of this envy?**
   Is this comparison leading to peace and purpose — or is it stirring up bitterness and burnout?

7. **Can I cheer her on without feeling like I'm falling behind?**
   What if I chose to celebrate her win...*and* trust that God's still writing a beautiful story for us too?

The Only Filter You Need

If you need a filter for your homeschool life, use this one:

- Grace for the messy days.
- Gratitude for the good days.
- Grit for the hard days.
- God's perspective for *every* day.

Because at the end of this journey, it won't be the curated snapshots that matter.

It'll be the hearts you raised.
The faith you modeled.
The memories you made.
The courage you lived out loud.

Even if your floors were sticky and your hair looked like you survived a hurricane.

CHAPTER 15:

Permission Slips You Didn't Know You Needed

Yes, You Can Take a Day Off.
Yes, You Can Change Plans.

If you've made it this far, you've probably figured out:
I'm basically the Oprah of homeschool permission slips.

"You get a permission slip!"
"And you get a permission slip!"
"EVERYBODY GETS A PERMISSION SLIP!"

Because here's the thing:
Most of us don't need more guilt.
We need more *grace*.

We don't need tighter schedules and stricter rules.
We need someone to look us in the eye and say:

"Hey. It's okay.
You're allowed to breathe."

So consider this chapter a giant, glitter-covered stack of permission slips you didn't even know you needed.

Real-Life Permission Slips You Actually Need

- ✅ You have permission to take the whole month of December off and call it "Christmas School." Baking cookies counts as chemistry. Watching *Home Alone* counts as a study in cause and effect. Extra credit if you quote Kevin McCallister.

- ✅ You have permission to stop mid-math when your best friend texts, "Let's take the kids to the zoo today," and you say YES.
  Spoiler: Feeding a giraffe counts as a life science field trip.

- ✅ You have permission to change curriculums mid-year, mid-month, mid-Tuesday if it's not working anymore.
  Double points if you change it while eating ice cream directly from the carton.

- ✅ You have permission to ditch the formal schedule for a week and just... read.
  Couch forts, endless books, and cereal for dinner? Educational gold.

- ✅ You have permission to travel the world with your kids.

And if you're going somewhere cool, please remember your favorite sarcastic homeschool author and pack me in your suitcase.

- [x] You have permission to call an ice cream bar "dinner" sometimes.
  (It's called "calcium enrichment." Fight me.)

- [x] You have permission to leave the kids with someone you trust, take a book, and go sit by a pool ALONE without guilt.
  Self-care is part of your homeschool plan. Look it up.

- [x] You have permission to wear pajamas until 2 p.m., survive on popsicles, and call it a "life skills day."
  Because surviving chaos is a life skill, friends.

- [x] You have permission to say no to the homeschool co-op, no to the enrichment classes, no to the field trips, and no to anything else that makes you want to crawl under your table and cry.
  Freedom is holy.

- [x] You have permission to be human.
  To be tired.
  To need a minute.
  To not have all the answers.

- [x] You have permission to REST without apology.

Chill Out, Friend

Homeschooling isn't about perfection.
It's not about having a bullet-journal schedule, a

hand-poured soy candle burning at all times, and laminated Latin flashcards neatly displayed next to your organic sourdough starter.

Although if that's your thing, you go, Glen Coco.

Homeschooling is about:

- Real life
- Real kids
- Real learning
- Real grace

It's about showing up with what you have, where you are, and trusting that God fills in the gaps.

Let me save you the suspense:
There will always be gaps.
There will always be grace for the gaps.

Your Job is Faithfulness, Not Performance

You are not being graded on how perfect your day looks.

You are not being judged on whether your house could be featured in *Better Homes and Homeschoolers* magazine.

You are not being weighed and measured by whether your kids finish every workbook page by May 15th.

You are being called to faithfulness.

- To show up.
- To love well.
- To learn alongside your kids.
- To model grace, grit, and perseverance — even when you're low-key, losing your mind.

Homeschooling is not a performance.

It's a calling.

And guess what?
God doesn't call you to it and then stand back with a clipboard waiting to catch your mistakes.

He walks with you through the whole messy, beautiful, pajama-clad journey.

Final Permission Slip (Framed and Signed)

Here it is:

You have permission to live this homeschool life fully, freely, and faithfully.

Not perfectly.

Not Pinterest-ly.

Not performance-based.

Just faithful. Just you.
Messy bun, Dr Pepper in hand, brain firing on caffeine, prayers, and sheer stubborn love.

You have permission to be a little bit feral today...
and call it homeschooling.

(And honestly? It's probably the best kind.)

CHAPTER 16:

The Real Goal of All of This

Raising Thinkers, Dreamers, Doers, and Disciples

Well, here we are.
The last official chapter.
And if you've made it this far without throwing the book across the room or hiding under a blanket...
you're my kind of people.

Before you close this book, stuff it under your couch cushions, and get ambushed by real life again —
I need you to know one last thing:

Homeschooling isn't really about spelling tests, math facts, science projects, or even transcripts.

It's about who you're raising.

Why We Really Do This

You're not homeschooling to raise kids who can recite the periodic table from memory.
Although, shoutout if you do. That's impressive.

You're homeschooling to raise:

- Thinkers — kids who know how to wrestle with ideas, ask real questions, and chase after real answers.

- Dreamers — kids who still believe that big dreams are worth dreaming…because nobody trained them to settle.

- Doers — kids who know how to get back up when they fall, who aren't afraid to try, build, fail, fix it, and try again.

- Disciples — kids who hear God's voice louder than the world's noise, who walk in grace and truth, who choose the narrow road when it would be easier to sit down on the wide one.

That's the goal.

Not perfect grades.
Not perfect transcripts.
Not perfect performances.

Faithful living.
Faithful thinking.
Faithful loving.

That's the real win.

You're Not Just Building Students.

You're Building Souls.

The goal isn't just to raise kids who can ace every pop quiz.
It's to raise kids who can stand when no one else will.

It's to raise humans who know why they believe what they believe.

Humans who think deeply, love wildly, speak truth boldly, and serve faithfully.

Humans who are willing to climb mountains, walk through valleys, fight for justice, love the broken, and shine bright when the world gets darker.

Homeschooling gives you the time, the space, the conversations, and the margin to build that.

One messy math lesson.
One long afternoon.
One deep car ride conversation at a time.

Homeschooling Isn't About Control.

It's About Calling.

You're not homeschooling because you think you can control every outcome.

If you've homeschooled for more than five minutes, you already know how funny that idea is.

You're homeschooling because you were called.

Called to plant seeds, you might not see bloom for years.
Called to build a foundation when no one else is watching.
Called to walk faithfully, even when it's slow, messy, and feels like everyone else is running ahead without you.

Homeschooling isn't about getting to write a "perfect" story.

It's about getting to be part of a holy one.

It's not about producing the smartest kid in the room.

It's about walking with your kids into a life that honors God, chases truth, and shines His light wherever they go.

Even when it's hard.
Even when it's messy.
Even when it's pajama days and burned science experiments and melted-down moments, where you wonder if you're even making a difference.

You are.

Final Words From My Heart

If you don't remember anything else from this book, remember this:

You don't have to homeschool perfectly.
You don't have to parent perfectly.
You don't have to *be* perfect.

You are already equipped — because He is with you.

You are already qualified — because He called you.

You are already enough — because He is enough.

> "You just have to be faithful.

Raise thinkers.
Raise dreamers.
Raise doers.
Raise disciples.

And trust God with the rest.

You are doing holy work—

Even on the days you feel like you're doing none of it right.
Even when no one else sees the effort.
Even when you doubt yourself.

God sees.
God knows.
God is working.

And one day, when you watch your kids step into the world with courage, wisdom, kindness, and grit…
You'll know:

It was worth it.
Every hard day.
Every late night.
Every pajama morning.
Every tear.
Every prayer.
Every step.

It was all building something bigger than you could see.

And just in case you needed the reminder one more time:

You don't have to wear a denim jumper to homeschool. (But if you want to, bestie? Rock it. Pockets are amazing.)

Extras:

A Letter to the Homeschool Mom Who's Still Not Sure

(Because You Might Need to Hear It Twice)

Hey, friend.

If you're holding this book, still flipping through these pages, still wondering if you're really cut out for this... I want you to lean in close for a minute.

Because I need you to hear something loud and clear:

You are not alone.

You're not the only one second-guessing.
You're not the only one who feels the tug... and the terror.
You're not the only one who lies awake at night asking,
"Am I enough?"
"Will I ruin them?"
"What if I can't do this?"

You're not crazy for loving your kids enough to even ask those questions.

You're braver than you feel right now.

If you're scared... it means you care.

If you're worried... it means you're paying attention.
If you're overwhelmed... it means you know the weight of what's at stake.

But none of that disqualifies you.
It *qualifies* you.

Because guess what?

The best teachers aren't the ones with the most polished lesson plans or the prettiest bulletin boards. The best teachers are the ones who show up — messy, real, human — and love their students enough to keep trying even when it's hard.

And nobody — nobody — loves your kids like you do.

You don't have to be fearless.

You just have to be faithful.

You don't have to have all the answers.
You just have to keep asking the right questions.

You don't have to be perfect.
You just have to be present.

You don't have to build a "perfect homeschool" from day one — or ever.
You just have to build a life worth learning in.

A life where love matters more than test scores.
A life where questions are welcome and wonder is contagious.
A life where faith is woven into the ordinary days and messy middles.

It's okay if you're scared.

It's okay if you're not sure yet.
It's okay if you need a minute — or a month — or a full summer to step out in faith.

There's no timer ticking down.
There's no magic deadline you missed.
There's just today — and the invitation God might be whispering into your heart:

"Trust Me with this too."

Not because you have all the qualifications.
Not because you have the perfect plan.
But because He knows what He planted in you — and what He planted in your kids.

He knows the way you'll grow together.

And whether you decide to homeschool or not...

You are not failing.
You are not too late.
You are not missing out on God's plan.

You are walking faithfully — one scared, brave step at a time.

And no matter what path you take,
He's already gone ahead of you.

You can trust Him.
You can trust yourself.
You can trust the story He's writing.

And yes — you can do it in pajamas if you want to.

Cheering for you always,

Lauren

Rapid-Fire FAQ

(Because You Might Still Wonder...)

Q: Do I need a homeschool room?
A: Nope. Kitchen table. Couch. Back porch. Front seat of the truck. Wherever learning happens, that's school.

Q: Can we stay in pajamas all day?
A: Not only can you... you might *thrive* in pajamas. Highly recommend.

Q: What if I mess up?
A: You will. You're still qualified. Grace > Guilt.

Q: How much math do we really have to do?
A: Enough to navigate life like a functioning adult. And maybe enough to impress a Chick-fil-A cashier with quick mental math.

Q: Can I work and homeschool?
A: Yes. It's not always easy, but it's absolutely possible. Creativity > Perfection.

Q: What if my kid wants to go to college?
A: They absolutely can — homeschoolers get in every year, many with scholarships. Your kitchen table diploma holds more weight than you think.

Q: What about socialization?
A: They'll be socialized. Some days, maybe too socialized. You'll be fine. They'll be fine. Even the chickens will be fine.

Q: Do I have to teach every subject every day?
A: Nope. You can loop, stack, batch, flex, and pivot. Homeschool life = real life.

Q: Am I enough for this?
A: Short answer: Yes.
Long answer: Yes, because God equips those He calls — even on the days you feel like you're building the ark without blueprints.

Q: What if my kid learns differently?
A: Congratulations. You just found one of the best reasons to homeschool: tailoring education to fit *them* — not the other way around.

Q: How structured should I be?
A: As structured as your sanity allows...and as flexible as real life demands.

Q: Will I ruin my kid if we have a hard year?
A: Nope. Hard years grow strong humans. (And strong moms & dads.)

Q: Is it normal to want to quit sometimes?
A: Normal, expected, and absolutely not disqualifying. Breathe, pray, adjust, and carry on.

Q: Do I have to finish every book we start?
A: No. Sometimes quitting halfway through is the wise move.

Q: Can I homeschool if I'm not super organized?
A: You can. You will. And you'll find systems (or hacks) that fit you better along the way.

Q: What about testing? How will I know they're learning?
A: Tests can help, but real learning shows up in conversations, curiosity, and growth — not just Scantron sheets.

Q: Should I have a daily schedule posted?
A: Only if it helps *you*. Otherwise? Sticky notes, mental lists, and "winging it with purpose" are all valid homeschool strategies.

Q: Will my kids be weird?
A: First of all, define "weird." Second, the world needs more kids who are kind, curious, and courageous — even if they grow up liking obscure hobbies and building epic backyard forts.

Q: What if I start and realize I hate it?
A: Then you pivot, adjust, pray hard, maybe cry a little, and find a version that fits better. Homeschooling has more gears than a mountain bike.

Q: How early is too early to start homeschooling?
A: Learning starts at birth. *Formal* homeschooling starts whenever you want. Spoiler: reading good books, going outside, and building block towers counts.

Q: Do I have to join a co-op?
A: Nope. It can be great if you want it — but you're not less legit without one.

Q: What if I'm bad at math?
A: Welcome to the club. God made tutors, videos, and friends who text you fractions answers for a reason.

Q: Can we take breaks? Even long ones?
A: 100%. Life is learning, too. Breaks breathe fresh life into tired minds.

Q: What about high school credits?
A: You can track them. You can build a transcript. You

can graduate your kid. Yes, even if you sometimes forget what day it is.

Q: How do I know if it's working?
A: Are they growing? Are they asking better questions? Are you having conversations you never would have had if they were gone all day?
That's how you know.

Q: What if my house is a mess and dinner is frozen pizza?
A: Then welcome to the real homeschool life, friend. You're doing it beautifully.

Acknowledgments

First and foremost, I give all glory and thanks to God, who has guided every step of this journey and filled me with the courage, wisdom, and grace to write these words. Without Him, none of this would be possible.

To my husband, thank you for being my rock, my biggest cheerleader, and my voice of reason when I needed it most. You have encouraged me through every doubt, picked up the slack when I was knee-deep in writing, and reminded me (more than once) to eat something besides Dr. Pepper and adrenaline. You believe in me even when I struggle to believe in myself. This book would not exist without your love and support. I am so grateful to walk this life and this homeschooling adventure by your side.

To my two amazing kids, you inspire me every single day. You remind me why this journey matters and why it is worth every moment. Watching you learn and grow is my greatest joy and the heartbeat behind these pages.

To my dad, thank you for being the one who first made me believe I had something worth writing. You cheered me on before there was anything to cheer for, listened to half-finished thoughts like they were polished ideas, and always reminded me that words have weight. You taught me to think deeply, speak carefully, and write bravely. So much of who I am—and why I write—traces back to you. This one's for you.

To Meagan Dedmon, thank you for being my sounding board, my fellow dreamer, and my steady friend through the rollercoaster of deciding to homeschool. You have listened to every wild idea, cheered me on when I doubted myself, and read through the drafts of this book. You have been my unofficial editor and therapist, and I could not have done this without you.

And finally, to every reader, thank you for picking up this book. I hope it encourages you, makes you laugh, and reminds you that you do not have to fit a mold to thrive in this homeschooling adventure.

www.ingramcontent.com/pod-product-compliance
Lightning Source LLC
Chambersburg PA
CBHW070150100426
42743CB00013B/2872